TANGLED
DESTINIES

A clash of cultures

A miraculous
love story

A message of hope
triumphs loss

JOHANNA GARRISON

Tangled Destinies
© 2015 by Johanna Garrison

Published by Insight International, Inc.
contact@freshword.com
www.freshword.com
918-493-1718

Scripture quotation is taken from the King James Version of the Bible.

This updated and expanded version was originally published in 1981
by Alton Garrison Ministries, Inc.

ISBN: 978-1-890900-93-9
E-book ISBN: 978-1-890900-94-6

Library of Congress Control Number: 2014947998

Printed in the United States of America

Endorsements

"*Tangled Destinies* is a *must* read for the dreamer that lives inside each of us. From the hardships of an overwhelmingly painful family history to the victory of renewed faith that God alone gives to individuals and families, *Tangled Destinies* provides the hope for you to believe for your miracle and the ability to achieve your dreams through Christ. Johanna and Alton are lifelong friends who are living out the pages of this book into a beautiful tapestry of love, promise, and redemption. Enjoy each minute you read because the dreamer inside you has been waiting for this book."

—Tommy Barnett
Co-Pastor, Phoenix First Assembly
Founder, Los Angeles Dream Center
Author of *Reaching Your Dreams* and *Multiplication*

"*Tangled Destinies* is absolutely captivating! I couldn't put it down. The stories of Henk Rijfkogel from Holland and a Chinese girl named Jan Nio Oei are woven together in a way that only a loving God could design. As you read about His sovereign work in their lives, you will be challenged to recognize His hand in your own journey. And their obedient faith will encourage you to depend on Him no matter how difficult your current circumstances might be. I know I'll be recommending this book again and again to my family, friends, and those I've yet to meet who will be encouraged by such an amazing picture of the beautiful way God shapes our lives for His glory."

—Kerry Clarensau
Director of a 340,000-plus-member national women's organization
Author of *Secrets: Transforming Your Life and Marriage, Love Revealed, Redeemed!*, and *A Beautiful Life*

Contents

Foreword

A friend of mine told me that there are no coincidences in life, only God-incidents. Is that true, or is life a sixty-yard dash with a brick wall for a finish line?

Are Christians overly glib when they recite Romans 8:28 as evidence God is working good in all things? Could that possibly be true?

Here is a book that answers those questions. It's a book that, once you begin reading, you will not be able to lay down.

Henk Rijfkogel was a teenager in Holland in World War II when an Allied plane flew overhead. As he watched, it dropped a bomb on their houseboat, instantly killing his mother, his sister, and her friend. All that he recovered of his mother's body was her scalp floating on the water. Understandably, he shook his fist at God.

You might have done the same thing. "Where was God in all this?" you ask. Sometimes our circumstances seem to shout at us that God is either absent or blind and powerless.

Young Henk was subsequently captured by Nazis, escaped, and after the war went off to fight for the Dutch to quell the Sukarno independence movement in Indonesia.

There he met Jan, a young woman from a strict Chinese home. She grew up in a Buddhist family and knew firsthand the presence and power of evil spirits. It should not have happened—the chance meetings between Henk and Jan—but, love blossomed over time. They married and shortly afterward the Dutch were forced out of Indonesia. Henk took his new bride and went back to Holland.

Jan found herself in a world she did not know. Within a year upon their arrival, their first of seven children was born. The marriage became very rocky, filled with strife, and the manifest presence of evil was assaulting Jan and filling her with terror.

Was there any hope for her? For this marriage? For the future of this family? A husband and father filled with anger? A wife and mother cracking under the strain of a new life and the ominous presence of evil? Could God work good in this?

In these pages you will read the miraculous deliverance that came to Henk and Jan. The story is told by their oldest daughter, Johanna. She is the wife of my dear friend and associate in ministry, the assistant general superintendent of the Assemblies of God, Alton Garrison. I urge you to keep some tissue with you as you read this book. There are moments when you will cry over the adversity described, and then later you will cry with joy over what the Lord did.

You will read of trial and tragedy, but you will also experience miracles of God's grace and power.

Tangled Destinies reminds me of the time when Corrie ten Boom spoke to audiences. She would hold up a piece of embroidered cloth, first showing the beauty of the embroidered side, with all the threads forming a beautiful picture, which she described as God's plan for our lives. Then she would flip over the cloth to show the tangled, confused underside, illustrating how we view our lives from a human standpoint. Finally, she would recite the poem of the weaver:

My life is but a weaving, between my God and me,

I do not choose the colors, He worketh steadily.

Oftimes He weaveth sorrow, and I in foolish pride,

Forget He sees the upper, and I the underside.

Not 'til the loom is silent and the shuttles cease to fly

Will God unroll the canvas and explain the reason why.

The dark threads are as needful in the Weaver's skillful hand

As the threads of gold and silver in the pattern He has planned.

(Author Unknown)

You will see those multicolored threads in the story Johanna has woven about her family. Their story is unique, but the truth is enduring for all. Take this book as an encouragement that God is also working for the good in your life, in your family. Hold on to that. Even in your darkest hours, God will never abandon you. He is for you.

Then, after you've read this book, take some moments to reflect on your own life. What were the dark places? How did the Lord bring you through? And, if you're not yet through that desert time in your life, can you tell the Lord that you have faith in Him regardless? Will you dare to believe that God has purpose and destiny in your life as well?

Finally, you will want to pass this book on to others. Do you know someone going through a rough patch? Order this as a gift for them. *Tangled Destinies* is not fiction—it's the real story of how God is always for us, even when life turns against us!

—Dr. George O. Wood
General Superintendent, Assemblies of God

PART I:

THE TANGLING

SCAN THE QR CODE OR

ENTER THE ADDRESS

IN YOUR WEB BROWSER

TO WATCH LIZETTE NENE,

JAN'S GRANDDAUGHTER,

INTRODUCE THE STORY OF HER FAMILY.

WWW.TANGLEDDESTINIES.COM/VIDEOS/1

1

Extinguished

The rumbling began about ten.

Sunday, September 17, 1944, was a clear, mild day along the Rhine River, with the sun reflecting happily off the decks of the dozens of houseboats tied up along the banks.

In one of them lived a mother with her son and daughter, and today, the daughter's girlfriend was visiting from town. The two girls were preparing Sunday dinner with the mother. The son was engrossed in a newspaper.

As the rumbling began, the boy glanced up from the page with a curious look on his face. The mother and the girls stopped their puttering at the stove and the table and cocked their heads to listen.

In the sky to the west was the unmistakable drone of airplanes. Many airplanes.

The four walked off the boat along the narrow gangplank to the shore, the boy peering intently into the sky, the ladies chattering quietly. Some of the neighbors, who were following the war more closely, had said the Allies were about to launch a major thrust in the Netherlands—but others had said no, General Patton was going to march up to Berlin from the South, and the Netherlands would be liberated later.

It was simple, in the boy's mind, to deduce that the planes they could now hear were indeed Allied aircraft and not Luftwaffe. The German air force would naturally fly from the east—if they could fly at all. The Luftwaffe was known to be decimated after a summer of ferocious confrontations with British and American flyers.

The women lasted only a few moments, then the empty sky bored them and their dinner preparations beckoned. The boy wandered back into the houseboat behind them, unable to see any planes. Perhaps he was mistaken.

No. As he sat back down in the houseboat, the continuing dull roar convinced him: aircraft were coming. While his mother and sister and the other girl talked on, rattling their kitchen utensils, oblivious for the moment to the Second World War, the boy walked back out of the houseboat, back down the gangplank onto land.

Soon, if he squinted, he could make out tiny specks just off the horizon, like grounds of tea floating in slow motion in the bottom of a cup. Then, as he shielded his eyes from the sun overhead, the specks took their inevitable shape, finally coming into plain view and roaring overhead.

They were Allied planes, signaled by the prominent star on each fuselage. The boy was not inclined to wave madly at the pilots, like so many Dutch who were already showing up in American newsreels. Instead, for the boy, it was a grim sight. Here came the liberating Allies, by his count more than two years late. It had been that long since his father's bloody clothes were shipped back from Germany.

The boy stood in his stocking feet with his back to the river, his hands in his pockets, leaning back to look up at the aircrafts' underbellies as they roared over him. There were certainly enough of them.

In a single instant, without warning, a furious blow threw him on his face. The monstrous noise and fiery wing of an explosion crushed him into the earth. Wood splinters and hot droplets of river water pelted his back and legs as the roar of the explosion echoed away from him.

Before he could lift his head he realized that other explosions were occurring up and down the river, that bombs were dropping, screaming as they descended, all along both banks. Buildings all around him were collapsing in heaps of rubble. The boy pulled his head and shoulders out of the dirt until he could see the river over his shoulder with one eye. The surface was churning; smoke and fire were pouring into the sky.

Suddenly he jerked his head up. Behind him was the little docking cubicle for the houseboat. The boy's eyes narrowed and his face pulled tight into the gritty corners of his mouth.

The houseboat was gone.

Two gnarled posts marked the place where the gangplank had begun at the shore and run out to the boat. The gangplank had been destroyed as well.

The boy threw himself onto his feet and hurdled to the water's edge as the Allied planes flew on their way, dropping bombs further and further up the Rhine. Here, in the aftermath, tiny scraps of deck and roof and kitchen floated helplessly down the river, spinning into the debris of a dozen other house-boats. Wailing and screaming cut through the hot air as the dead were discovered and the injured begged for discovery.

The boy's sister and her friend were completely annihilated. As his eyes searched through the ghastly remains of the houseboat community along the river's edge, he found only a scrap of his mother's scalp, with a shred of her hair still attached—and he retrieved her Bible, floating alone in the midst of horror. That was all.

No tears came to the boy's eyes. The anger that choked his gut would not accommodate tears. He felt the fury pulling his insides tight as his eyes locked in on that shameful remnant of his precious mother.

Here before him lay the awful remains of his life. His father murdered by the Axis Powers—his mother and sister destroyed inexplicably by the Allies.

The boy's fist clenched hard. He stood on the edge of the Rhine and gritted his teeth and shook a fist in God's face.

"You're no God to me!" he shouted hoarsely over the water, into the dust-thickened sky. "To let this good family be wiped out! Damn you! You're no more God than I am!"

And yet, as he trudged away from the river in his town stockings, two startling facts would give him pause, even in his fury. First, the building beside which he had been thrown by the explosion was the only building left standing in the attack. Second, he was the only survivor of Looveer, the once-quaint little string of houseboats.

The boy proceeded to bury as many of the dead as he would find. He was too stupefied to take shoes from one of the corpses to replace his own lost pair. Finally he stalked away, alone, with no material possessions whatsoever, and no blood relatives save one: his lost brother, who had fled from the Nazis long ago.

SCAN THE QR CODE OR

ENTER THE ADDRESS

IN YOUR WEB BROWSER

TO WATCH SAM RIJFKOGEL

EXPLAIN HOW TO RESPOND

WHEN YOU HAVE LOST EVERYTHING.

WWW.TANGLEDDESTINIES.COM/VIDEOS/2

2

Children of
Different Worlds

All the waters of the Asian world poured into Jakarta in 1929.

Walking into the steamy streets were not only the native Indonesians but Dutch and Chinese as well, each with their own package of customs, each with their own cultural and social system—separate, yet strangely and inevitably intertwined.

The dark-skinned Indonesians, whose home these islands truly were, dominated Jakarta by a wide percentage, and provided the somewhat loose, handshaking happy island atmosphere. They seemed to worship virtually anything they could, from trees to rocks to waterfalls—to their ancestors.

But the quiet, stiffer Chinese, many whose parents and grandparents had left their homeland in boats to make new lives in the islands, formed another piece of the population pie. They could be counted on for commerce, their keen business instincts motivating the economy of the Indonesian cities. They reverenced Buddha, and, in times of special stress, the spirits of the netherworld.

And the pale Dutch, looking so strangely out of place with their blond hair and European uniforms, patrolled the ports and controlled the rubber plantations with the quiet pomp of kindly foreign masters, a role they had played for over three hundred years. The Dutch had lived there for generations, and yet they had never truly mixed. The Knil—the island-born Dutch, most of whom were career military—had their own compounds, away from the Indonesian and Chinese populations. Most of the Europeans were starchy Dutch Reformed by religious tradition, and some were Catholic.

Most of the Indonesians and Chinese felt favorably disposed toward the Dutch—protection from Asian predators and freedom to squeeze out a simple living were their only requirements, and the Dutch had faithfully provided both for three centuries. Too, the Dutch had brought from western Europe such modern innovations as cobblestone streets, sanitation and education. The Dutch Reformed Church and the Catholics as well had set up churches and schools.

All of which existed in tandem with the trappings of pagan worship, the strongest religious force in the islands. It was for the sake of the gods that players entertained on street corners wearing bamboo horse costumes or gruesome masks, exercising in the occult, eating glass and foaming at the mouth and promoting their favorite deities to passersby. Occult games were organized at major intersections—anyone could play. Some sects sold flowers that were supposed to please the gods on certain days of the week, burning them with a putrid incense that the Dutch called *wierook* and the Indonesians called *kemenyan*. Sometimes they cut strips of banana tree to burn with the concoction, scenting each doorpost in their houses—all for the safety of the inhabitants of the house.

But there were dangers in this land of mixed religions as well. One example: anyone crossing the path of a Muslim on his way to the temple, it was said, would die a horrible death.

Into one of the proper Chinese homes that year was born a proper Chinese baby, a girl, given the proper Chinese name Jan Nio Oei in the ancient Buddhist tradition. Her father sighed. Now, in fifteen or sixteen years, he could worry about her getting in trouble. The Chinese rarely intermarried with either the Dutch or the Indonesians—all three groups maintained strict separate racial identities—but the Dutch-soldier boys loved to seduce the Chinese girls. The Indonesian girls, without the rigid social fiber of the Chinese—no dancing, no boyfriends for the Chinese girls—were less of a challenge to them.

At the age of six, Jan was enrolled in kindergarten in the Chinese school, something the Chinese people had established for themselves. The following year her younger brother Tik Kie began there too. He excelled. She did not. She was bored by the Buddhism lessons and confused by the Chinese lessons. Even with Chinese blood, she had grown up speaking Indonesian with her friends, and hearing Dutch on the streets.

The Dutch had also established a school for Chinese children, where they could learn Dutch. It was a Catholic school, but many Chinese parents sent their children there to learn the language without realizing that they were also being schooled in the Catholic religion.

Here, little Jan was enchanted. Every morning the class would stand and pray. At times each week the teachers would lead the children to the sanctuary in the center of the school building. Wide eyed, Jan would dip her hand in the holy water and kneel. At the front of the room was a large statue of a man the Catholics called Jesus, hanging on a cross. It might have been a gruesome thing, except that Jan had never encountered death before, and the hanging man to her simply seemed vulnerable, the object of so much affection. Every time Jan knelt before it she was strangely moved. Something inside warmed to that man hanging there. She looked around and saw nuns, black-clad and reverent, bowing silently before him. Every day, without fail, the Catholics knelt solemnly—while Jan's parents in the Buddhist tradition, rarely visited the temple more than twice a year, unless they had some specific problem that required speedy action by the gods.

There was a gap for little Jan, a chasm between the faiths of East and West that made her vaguely uncomfortable. The devotion of the Catholics appealed to her—they had something inside that she didn't have. She didn't see them nervously leaving offerings of food and incense in little pots at every doorpost inside their houses every night to ward off evil spirits, as the Chinese and Indonesians did, to protect themselves and their belongings.

If she could, Jan decided, she would become a Christian someday. But she better not tell her parents.

After three years of Catholic school, Jan's parents pulled her out of school, leaving Tik Kie behind in his academic successes. Education was high on their Chinese list of priorities. But the Catholic school was expensive, and the Oei family was growing by a brother or sister every year or so. World War Two had broken out, and money was very tight. Many children in Indonesia abruptly stopped going to school as the Japanese began threatening the Asian islands.

Still, in her mind, Jan often saw that man hanging on the cross before her. And she liked him.

~~~

Half a world away, with the war to end all wars behind them, Europeans enjoyed the 1920s with rare exuberance. Full of hope for a carefree future, many families added to their ranks by making babies gleefully. Before long, with the world gone sour once again, those same babies would flee for their lives before Hitler's slavemongers.

The Rijfkogel family, living in Hasselt, near Overijssel, spawned a daughter, Boukje, and two sons, John and Henk, as their contribution to the baby boom. The boys grew healthy and strong and good-looking, in the likeness of their father.

As the Germans began their advance on western Europe, German soldiers began raiding such Dutch villages as Hasselt and Overijssel, carrying off the strongest men to work in the German forced-labor factories. The Rijfkogel boys were barely teenagers when their father was seized by the Germans and taken away.

He simply failed to come home for dinner one evening. Mrs. Rijfkogel began to fear the worst when he was only a few minutes late. Word flashed through town like electricity—the Nazis had come to the railroad depot where Rijfkogel worked. The entire shift was arrested and driven away in big German trucks. Nothing was said to the victims' families—but then, nothing ever was.

Mrs. Rijfkogel, a strong-willed Christian woman, disintegrated as she listened to the neighbor tell what he had heard. She was blind in one eye, but she could see the future all too clearly—her husband's coarse stubbornness would destroy him. She was a realist. She never had a moment of hope for him.

Young Boukje kept a pitiful count of the days her papa was gone. She had counted nearly to one hundred when a Red Cross representative interrupted supper by appearing at the door with a parcel in his arms. It was neatly tied in string. He reported solemnly that Rijfkogel had died of natural causes in service to the German Reich.

After he left, the three children circled their mother as she sat at the kitchen table and untied the package. She let out a short gasp as she opened the box. Inside were the clothes her husband had worn to work the day he disappeared. They were pasted with blood.

The gruesome grapevine eventually brought back the story. He had stubbornly refused to cooperate with the German taskmasters. Enraged, they had shot him to death.

The Germans continued their raids. Night after night, Jews were herded into trucks and driven away to unknown destinations. In whispers, the Dutch talked about mass exterminations in ovens, thousands of corpses littering concentration camps in the east.

And the kidnapping of Gentile Dutch males went on too. As the war dragged on, boys as young as sixteen were considered acceptable for duty in the factories of Germany. The same kind of trucks that transported the Jews transported the Gentile boys.

Grief spread like cancer from family to family as each household lost its sons. With each disappearance, Mrs. Rijfkogel grew more frantic.

It was finally decided that John, now seventeen years old, must join the Dutch underground, the resistance movement that provided, among other things, a network of risky hiding places and running routes for young Dutchmen.

There was someone in the neighborhood who had a contact with the underground who could help John get up to the northern part of Holland, where many farmers were willing to hide Dutch boys in their haylofts and attics during the dangerous daylight hours.

John Rijfkogel embraced his mother, his brother, and his sister, and slipped into the night sometime in 1941.

Money often became scarce for the Oei family, which eventually included ten children, and Jan Nio's father grew frustrated in his work because of it. He had worked for the same man as long as Jan could remember, but as the company grew, her father had gotten lost in the shuffle. He found it hard to gain any special recognition, and without the modern ascendancy of labor unions, he had not been given a raise in years.

Finally he decided to take action. He slipped a few coins into his pocket and left the house one evening to talk to a man who practiced *leyak*, or witchcraft. The medium burned a little incense, then asked Oei to explain the problem he was facing. The medium sat motionless. Behind his eyes, the mystical concoction was already being planned.

In a corner of the room sat an urn, full of dirt gathered from mummified corpses. The medium took a tiny linen pouch and sprinkled a little of the dirt into it, then tied it shut and handed it to his customer. Oei was to wear the pouch on his person at all times. Then the medium consulted his calendar and advised Oei to eat only one banana and drink only coffee on certain days each month.

The customer paid his twenty-one cents and left.

Soon Oei was bumping into the boss more and more frequently. They spent valuable time talking, and the employer's esteem grew for his longtime employee. Then came the salary increases, a chauffeur for the children's daily trips to and from school, the new clothes for the children, and eventually a new, larger house for the family.

Jan could see that black magic really worked—there was never really any question in her mind. But she did not like it, and she did not know why.

~~~

Henk, the baby of the Rijfkogel family, took over the reins of its leadership at the age of fifteen. With John gone to the underground, the family moved down the Rhine River to Looveer near Arnhem, where a doctor-friend agreed to rent them his houseboat, which was docked there in a whole little community of houseboats. The war was not so severe here, in the eastern part of Holland.

Henk sold himself convincingly to the ferrymaster, who carried commuters across the Rhine several times each hour. Soon Henk was running the ferry himself, ten hours a day. Winter was fierce. Many nights Henk's fingers ached from the cold. All year long the notorious Rhine fog made it treacherous work. On some nights Henk's mother hung a lantern outside their houseboat. Often Henk could only guide the ferry across by following the light.

But the Allies were planning an invasion.

—*mm*—

In Indonesia, Jan Nio Oei was able to enroll in nursing school in her hometown of Semarang while she was still a teenager. She devoted herself to her studies. The Dutch soldiers patrolling the area sometimes teased the other girls, but Jan always averted her eyes, and usually they left her alone.

The gods frowned on her family one day. Jan's younger sister Lian, three years old, ambled into the path of some Muslims who were making their way down the street to their temple. By the end of the day the little girl had taken a ferocious fever, and for hours she lay in delirium, foul-smelling fluids oozing out of her body. Her parents, who would normally have bolted to action, drooped into an enchanted sleep, powerless to help her. Only the following morning were they able to awake and act.

Jan's father went to the Chinese temple for a prescription. From there he hurried to the nearest pharmacy. They did not have the medicine called for in the prescription.

Meanwhile, Jan's mother called on the same mysterious gentle Indonesian man she had called on in times of trouble before. None of the children knew his name—or even his title—but when one of them was sick or there was some kind of trouble in the house, Mrs. Oei often summoned him. Many times he had Jan's mother fill a bowl with oil and onion pieces. Then he took the bowl outdoors, lifted it toward the heavens, and said a prayer to the gods. Back inside, he smeared the oil on the sick child—and invariably the child was well by the next day.

Today the Indonesian man went through the same ritual—but as he came back into the house he did not go toward Lian to anoint her. Instead he approached Mrs. Oei.

"She is not going to live," he said grimly. "I will anoint her anyway, but Lian is going to die."

A long time after the Indonesian man had gone, Jan's father returned, panicky and exhausted. He had hunted all over the city, stalking from pharmacy to pharmacy, but the medicine prescribed by the Chinese temple doctor was inexplicably out of stock in every store.

It was already too late anyway. The family had watched helplessly as Lian died, a victim of the hyperactive Indonesian occult.

⁓⁓⁓

In a world full of war, doctors and nurses become gods and goddesses. Demand for their services always outstrips supply when soldiers are filling operating rooms and wheelchairs by the hundreds every day.

As Japan and the other Axis powers squared off against Europe and the Allies, the Indonesian islands became a playground for the war games. Japan invaded, declared itself in control of the entire thirteen-thousand-island nation and thumbed its nose at the Dutch "protectors." Fighting in some parts of the country was vicious, but for the most part Indonesia was so far from both Japan and the Netherlands that neither suitor had time or resources to court her properly.

So it was more splendid patriotism than tough work, Jan Nio Oei discovered, to be a nurse in 1947. She was graduated from nurses' training and looked for a job in a Catholic institution, still flirting with the old longing to become a Christian.

She was hired at St. Elizabeth Hospital in Semarang to work the third floor under head nurse Groenwald in pediatrics.

This part of Indonesia was still held solidly by the Dutch, whose military personnel patrolled it fastidiously. Jan gradually developed a fascination for the Dutch sailors and soldiers.

There were rumblings in the mountains these days. People said a fellow named Sukarno, an Indonesian patriot, was amassing power—arms, ammunition, guerrillas—to seize control of the Indonesian nation in the wake of the confusion created by the World War squabbling.

Jan didn't understand that way of thinking at all. The Dutch were clearly a cut above. They were good people, they had been good protectors, good providers. There had never been an Indonesian army. How in the world could the Indonesians take over?

———

Henk headed north in his stocking feet through the woody *bossen* and the villages of Holland. He walked all afternoon into the deep of night. When cold and fatigue finally ground him to a stop, he knocked on the door of a farmhouse and begged for a place to stay. The lady of the house was helpful—she found an old pair of work shoes that her husband no longer wore and gave them to the wanderer.

After two cups of hot tea and some simple pastries, she led him to the stairway. On the wall at the base of the stairs he noticed a wooden plaque. "Do not go into the world alone," it read. "Take God with you."

Henk snorted cynically as he climbed the stairs to the guest room.

It took weeks to locate John. Information about the underground was always sketchy because no one could trust anyone else completely. The search ended in the attic of a warehouse.

John stood anxiously in the shadows, as he had learned to do during the past three years in hiding. One could never trust his host—let alone the visitor. Now, in the dim light of the attic, he could make out the features of his baby brother's face— features now more rugged, more hardened than he remembered. Henk, too, thought his brother had aged more than three years.

They embraced silently for a moment, then broke, each holding the other's forearms solidly in his grasp.

"How is Mama?" John asked with a steady, hopeful look in his eye.

Henk began to answer directly, then hesitated and looked away. He exhaled. He thought he would be tougher than this in the moment of truth.

"She's dead. Boukje too."

John looked to his left and spat. "The SS."

"No." Henk looked up at him tentatively. "The Allies. They bombed all along the Rhine just before the invasion. I hear they thought they were rousting out Nazis."

"The houseboat?"

"They demolished it. They were inside. Seven Sundays ago."

John sighed. "Did you bury them?"

"I'm sorry, John. I searched, but there was nothing left. They were gone."

John set his jaw and turned, as so many survivors inevitably did, to talk of the war in colder terms.

"Up here we heard the invasion failed."

"I left the day of the bombing. I've only heard bits and pieces. Someone said the Germans had held Arnhem Bridge, but they destroyed almost all of Arnhem in the process."

There was a long silence.

"God help us," John muttered. "We're all that's left of us."

Henk sat down on the cot with a thud.

"God has helped me more than I care to be helped," he replied evenly. "We're damn near extinguished."

Weeks later a package was handed off through the ranks of the Dutch underground and finally delivered to Henk. It was a roll of film. Among the photographs was one Henk had taken at the houseboat in Huissen, with his mother and sister and the girlfriend who had been killed with them. They were posing frivolously for the snapshot. The note with the package said that the film had been retrieved from the Rhine at Westervoort, miles below Huissen.

Henk was grateful, but the blessing was bittersweet.

The underground had none of the comedy that American television would later assign it. Henk and John spent their days hiding in haystacks and stables and attics, their nights eating scant, furtive meals with nervous host families and moving, moving, always trying to stay one step ahead of the vicious German Gestapo agents whose careers were built on the carcasses of rebellious Dutchmen.

Staying together was difficult. Many Dutch sympathizers could only hide one at a time. Eventually the brothers were forced to split up.

Henk skirted danger continually. For a time he smuggled downed Allied fighter pilots downriver in the false bottom of a grain barge. At other times, he was a fugitive himself.

Hiding in a barn one day, he heard German agents shouting at the owner. Desperate to create a diversion, Henk slipped the locking bar off the barn door and silently rounded up all the horses in the barn. At the door, he began punching their hind quarters to make them bolt out into the yard. As the owner went scrambling past the Germans, screaming at his galloping horses, Henk slipped out the back way and headed once again for the unfriendly bossen, the Dutch forests.

The odds caught up with him in Apeldoorn. There, Henk was captured along with several farmers in the area who were accused of harboring the likes of Henk. While Henk watched, the Germans gunned down the entire group of farmers. But Henk was young and strong. They could make good use of him.

As they marched him to their destination, collecting other prisoners along the way, Henk's mind raced furiously to come up with an escape plan. His chances were slim, but he could not escape the memory of his father's bloody clothes, and he knew survival was no more likely in captivity than in an escape attempt.

The group moved into a farmhouse for the night, and Henk watched for an opportunity to bolt for freedom. For a moment he was left alone, and he slipped out of the house. A German soldier caught him squarely as he crossed the threshold.

Punishment was instant and harsh. A hefty German thrashed the captive Dutchman with a rubber hose until he screamed in pain. Again and again, the heavy length of rubber bit into Henk's flesh, cutting across his back and sides, his arms and legs, and his head. Then the captors stood on Henk's hands and knees while another German dashed his arches repeatedly with a rifle butt trying to break Henk's feet. But the defiant Dutchman's bones would not snap.

Henk lay in a heap in the night, heaving with pain, only half-conscious. The next morning he was hurled to the floor and forced to stand up. The Nazis threw his shoes into the fireplace and forced him to continue the trek in his bare feet. Escape through the heavy snow would be more difficult that way.

But as he shuffled along, aching, alone, he kept watching for an opportunity to escape. Suddenly, as the group passed over a bridge in the remote forest, Henk slipped out of the company, down the bank, sliding into the icy water directly under the bridge.

The water was deathly cold, cutting like a razor into his wounds, and Henk's gums grew pale and his body convulsed as he held himself almost entirely under the surface, waiting for the Nazis to discover him. They came back to the area several times with flashlights and dogs. But Henk kept still. Eventually the foiled Germans gave up and moved on.

Finally, hours later, Henk dragged himself out of the river and into the winter woods. In a hollow log, draped in snow, he curled up and shivered himself to sleep.

And with the next day's sun, he trudged on, beaten but not broken.

3

Jungle Patrol

In the space of twenty-four months, the world deck was reshuffled and new hands were dealt to all players. Hitler and Mussolini arrived at their grisly ends, Roosevelt collapsed as victory approached. Truman bombed Japan. Stalin began playing his aces. The ragged Germans marched limply out of Holland. The sullen Japanese sailed out of Indonesia's ports.

But the prewar status quo, so striven for, did not return. That precious status quo was further gone from Holland than anywhere else. Their families and businesses ravaged, the rebuilding would be excruciating. But in the Pacific, their idyllic island colonies would throb painfully as well.

Sukarno, the hero of Indonesia's native people, had discovered the thrill of grassroots popularity and the power that can be had there when leadership is struggling. The cry of Sukarno's campaign, "Merdeka!" —freedom!—began to thump across the 13,677 islands of the chain. The ragged Dutch, nervous with the noise and tired of fighting, reluctantly held their wartime stance—such as it was, with their army in tatters—and began shipping more troops to Jakarta and other

Indonesian cities to maintain uneasy order. Recruiters in the Netherlands scrambled wearily to entice young men to sign up.

Soldiers arriving in Indonesia after the war found an odd mix of pressures represented by the armed forces there. The Dutch regulars who had come before them to fight the Japanese had a certain air of superiority—they had, after all, held Indonesia for the Dutch. The Knil, those Dutch by blood but Indonesian by birth, had a certain air of superiority—they were, after all, the dominating "tribe," the ones who had carved out a life in the jungle, so to speak, and who planned to stay on, generations after the Dutch soldiers had spent their enlistment terms and gone home to Holland. And now the Indonesians—the Sukarno-inspired natives—had an air of superiority that the Dutch had rarely encountered before…and that the Indonesians had rarely exercised before.

Only the Chinese Indonesians held their peace. They didn't like the tension. It was bad for business.

Guerrilla fighting had already broken out in the mountains and smaller cities by the time Henk Rijfkogel answered the recruiter's call. Bitter and alone after finishing out the European war in hiding, Henk enlisted and requested assignment in Indonesia. He had nothing holding him in Holland. Every village was a gnarled reminder of the mindless hell that had snuffed out his parents and his sister. He might as well shoot at some cocky Indonesians and see the world.

———

Jan Nio Oei shook her head whenever the lunchtime chatter turned to talk of the rebellion. She had grown up in a paradise, free of such complications, and had expected life to go on like this. At seventeen—almost eighteen—she had enough quandaries about life without the worries that Sukarno was creating. Every few weeks another bloody incident in the city forced her to confront the mess again—the Indonesians were forming an army called the TNI—and she did not like it.

Still, as a female in the big city, she was insulated from the tension in many ways. Women were discounted in the political struggle, and the rebellion flourished mainly in the outer reaches of the islands, where Dutch antiguerrilla units were fighting to maintain control.

Jan's life was still one of leisure. Occasionally she took a three-day weekend and helped Tan and Ida, friends of her family who owned a photography shop on Doewet Street there in Semarang. Jan was becoming reasonably skillful in development of snapshots. And it was fun.

The Dutch army, pulling itself up by the proverbial boot-straps, sent its Pacific-bound recruits to England for training because the war had decimated their own training facilities. Henk had never been outside Holland, but six months of England failed to fascinate him. The nation's capital, London, lay in a postwar shambles. Scotland was wasted less by bombs but more by the nagging economic stress of World War Two.

Henk could see the ugly side of almost anything these days.

A Dutch military plane droned across the Middle East and lower Asia to deposit him in Jakarta in 1946. This could have been exotic—a jungle nation, tropical and intriguing, a world away from the Continental propriety of Holland.

But Henk had only come to do a job, to put down a rebellion, to knock heads. He was not a tourist. He was not amused by the island ambience, the almost playful attitude that Indonesia's culture could have appeared to have.

Henk's tough exterior served him well in the armed forces. He was stationed in the mountains outside Jakarta, where rebel activity was on the rise, and placed in charge of an antiterrorist patrol. Antiterrorism by its nature must resort to the same tactics as its adversary, and Henk became skillful in the art of sabotage, stealth, and assassination.

As the leader of his patrol, Henk rode in the lead jeep as they scoured the mountains for guerrillas. Ambushes were common. His friends died around him almost day by day. Pain no longer seemed unusual, but the norm. Henk grew more and more calloused.

Then one day the lead jeep struck a land mine. The vehicle exploded into a million ragged fragments, the occupants thrown yards away in all directions. Henk was socked into the earth facedown, his body riveted by metal splinters and rocks—all in a gruesome reprise of the houseboat bombing.

He awoke in a military hospital, racked with pain, but steeped in a bitterness that made him sneer at the episode. He refused to be sedated as doctors plucked the hundreds of gritty pieces from his flesh and muscle. He had nothing to live for, and dying was just as absurd a concept to him by now.

And when he had recuperated, he thrust himself back into the jungle with a smoldering resolve.

Torture was a prime technique of Henk's patrol. When they suspected that an arsenal of weapons had been assembled by the guerrillas, they took one of the rebels prisoner and strapped one hand behind his back. Then they hung him by his twisted arm from the limb of a tree, and placed a land mine under him.

The guerrilla screamed in agony as his muscles and bones ripped and popped under his own weight—and he continued to pull back, to keep himself from dropping onto the mine. It took only a few minutes for the guerrilla to confess the location of the arsenal.

More than once Henk sneaked into enemy territory to count the guerrillas he would face in the combat of the next day.

Henk also became accustomed to the occult in the underbrush of Indonesia's jungles. When a fellow officer grew violently ill and doctors could not solve the case, Henk brought a spiritualist from the island of Ambon, a major center of leyak and black magic, to visit the patient.

The Ambonese man was direct.

"Have you slept with any local women?" he asked.

"Just one."

"Do you still sleep with her?"

"No."

"Is she happy about that?"

"No."

"Give me her name and address."

The Ambonese man went to the girl's house. No one was home. He went inside and found a mound of kemenyan, or incense. Apparently, it had been burning nonstop for several days. Around it were several of the officer's belongings—a handkerchief, a penknife. And there was a photograph of the man, peppered with the telltale pinpricks of voodoo.

The Ambonese man destroyed everything in the room and returned to report his findings to Henk and his friend.

The man began recovering the next day. He was out of the hospital within the week.

The spirit world became more and more a curiosity to Henk as his tour of duty in Indonesia stretched past months and into years. One of his few close friends was an Indonesian captain, whose great vice was boasting about his immortality in battle. Henk finally grew irritated by the claims and challenged his friend on the subject.

"What makes you think you can't be killed just like any of us?" he demanded.

The captain pulled a tiny pouch out of his pocket. It was full of dirt from mummified corpses.

"The witchdoctor gave me this before I joined the army," he replied with a wide grin. "It keeps me from all harm. No bullet will kill me as long as I carry this."

Henk snorted. "That's ridiculous."

The captain drew his revolver and held it out to Henk. "Try it."

Henk looked at him suspiciously. "That's your own gun," he responded after a moment's thought. "I'll try it with my gun."

"Go ahead," the captain chuckled.

The challenge made Henk angry. He knew if he killed the man he would be court-martialed and executed. But life had no value for him, and he let his fury carry him.

He pulled out his revolver and checked the chamber. It was full of bullets. He straightened his arm and fired at the man's chest. The bullet tore a circular hole in his shirt.

The man stood still, looking evenly at Henk.

Henk paused only a moment, then squeezed the trigger again and again, emptying the entire gun into his friend. Every bullet ricocheted away and disappeared, leaving only the ripped cloth as evidence.

~~~

Life was ugly in the jungle. When rations could not get through because of the fighting, Henk and his men killed monkeys and jungle birds, skinned them and cooked them over open fires.

When finally Henk drew leave, he headed for the city of Semarang. He would have company there. Henk's brother John had taken up the remnants of his life as a soldier as well. John had also been assigned to Indonesia, and now he would be leaving from Semarang for reassignment in Holland. Henk wanted to see him before his exit. He knew he might never see John again.

Fighting was ferocious as Henk passed through the battle zone toward Semarang. His jeep was ambushed in a thick jungle area. A guerrilla bullet smashed through the body of one of his companions. The jeep was mutilated by gunfire. Henk and the rest of the survivors dashed for cover, then picked their way through the underbrush to the next Dutch-held camp, where they picked up a new jeep and pressed onward without a break.

Henk arrived at the base in Semarang still covered with mud and blood. He walked up to John and said, "Are you Sergeant Rijfkogel?"

John looked up, surprised. "I am Rijfkogel, but not a sergeant." He did not know his brother.

Henk grinned. "I'm Henk."

It was a giddy reunion. Free from the turmoil of the war, far from the turmoil that their homeland represented, the two brothers reverted to their boyhood spirits and milked the city of Semarang for all the action it was worth. They gave each other an unbridled whirlwind tour of the area, with both of them snapping pictures all along the way, reason gleefully abandoned.

By the end of the third day, the brothers had spent countless rolls of film, rolls which they decided to drop off at a little camera shop in the commercial district of Semarang.

4

A Dapper Dutchman

They slammed open the flimsy screen door, joking and laughing, feeling very much the dapper Dutchmen in the uniforms. They paid practically no attention at all to the young Chinese girl behind the counter as she took down the name—"Rijfkogel," she printed carefully—and the address where the prints could be sent when they were finished.

But Henk had noticed her—noticed that the shop's manager had called her Jan from the back room, noticed that Jan was a beautiful, poised young lady with big dark eyes, prominent Chinese cheekbones, and a pretty mouth. As the brothers walked down the sidewalk, Henk said, "I'm going back there later. She's nice."

John was non-committal. "Chinese," he shrugged. "They're cliquish. Hard to get to know."

"Yes, but she's pretty."

John looked sideways at his brother. "I'm Dutch. I'd never marry one of those Chinese."

"Neither would I," Henk replied. "I'm just as Dutch. I may live here till I die, but I'd never marry a Chinese—or an Indonesian."

"So why go back?"

Now it was Henk's turn to shrug. "I like her." He knew the stores closed at 6:00 p.m. "I'm going back over there at 6:00 p.m. and take her home. Or wherever she wants to go."

"She's young. She may not want to go with you."

"She's old enough. We'll see. I bet I leave that shop with her."

Jan Nio Oei, according to her practice, kept an eye on the street as she finished her day's work. Her father would be coming soon on his bicycle to pick her up, just as he did each day. In the Chinese tradition, he was keenly protective of his daughter—especially with so many promiscuous Dutch soldiers roaming the streets.

Henk returned alone and took position across the street.

Six o'clock came and went, and Jan's father did not show. Sometimes he was delayed. Jan left the shop and headed down the sidewalk toward home.

Henk crossed the street toward her and fell into step alongside her.

"Good evening, Jan."

Jan's face grew rigid. She was startled that he knew her name. "What do you want?"

"Just to talk to you. I noticed you in the camera shop today."

She remembered him.

"So what do you want?"

Henk smiled. Chinese girls were known for this suspicious bent. "Just to take you to dinner. I just noticed you—"

"My father will be coming by any moment and you'll be in trouble and so will I."

"Oh, I wouldn't worry—"

"I would," Jan replied coolly. "Please don't walk with me." Inside she was scared—not of Henk, but of her father's reaction if he were to see her chatting with a Dutch soldier.

"All right," Henk sighed, dropping back a few steps. "Is this better?"

Jan grinned without turning around. "You're going to walk behind me?" It was amusing to her in a Chinese way. The Chinese women usually trailed their men this way in public.

"What's your full name?" Henk asked in a playful sing-song from behind her.

"Oh stop. My father will kill me."

Jan kept looking around, expecting to see the old man peddling up at any moment.

"Do you live around here?" Henk persisted gently.

Jan turned a corner. She needed to get onto the side streets if she wanted to spare herself her father's anger.

"You are very gracious in the camera shop," Henk offered. He was still following her by a few paces.

"Oh?" she responded flatly.

I am not interested in this person, she told herself. *I don't know who he is or what he's up to.*

And yet something inside of her proper Chinese being made an allowance for this odd stranger.

"How long have you worked there?" Henk went on.

"Mmm," Jan mumbled, her eyes still darting up and down the street.

"I haven't been back in Holland for years. I don't have any girlfriend here at all."

She wondered about this. Some soldiers were fond of making local girls feel sorry for them.

"Is that so?" she asked.

"Yes, I'd only like to be your friend," Henk replied simply.

She took note of this tone. She believed him.

"This intersection is too close," she broke in. "My house is just up there. My father will be watching for me."

"All right."

He stopped walking. She kept going, but she stopped after a couple steps and turned around.

"Why did you wait for me outside the shop and follow me all this way?" she asked.

Henk looked at her intently. Some guard within him had been lowered. Logic had fled the scene.

"Because I love you," he said.

She looked at him—a Dutch soldier in his early twenties, perhaps a better actor than most Dutch soldiers, but a Dutch soldier nonetheless.

"Certainly," she replied and turned around. She did not look back again.

She did not think any more about him that evening.

In the hottest part of the day, business was prone to slow down. The next afternoon found Jan and Ida, the manager's wife, standing in front of the shop, relaxing in the lull.

Before long Henk was approaching, walking casually up the street. Jan saw him coming and expected him to speak. She braced herself for the inevitable explaining she would have to do for the benefit of her employer's wife.

Henk meanwhile saw the woman talking with Jan and decided not to create a problem for her. When he got to the shop, he walked right on by, without a word.

Jan felt herself growing angry at the brush-off. She didn't mention it to Ida, but privately she decided to do something about it. No Dutch soldier was going to make a fool of her.

Inside the shop, she thumbed through her orders and came up with Henk's name and address. She recopied the information on a separate sheet of paper and tucked it into a pocket. She would deal with him later.

The next day was the end of Henk's leave. He went to port and saw his brother off. Henk returned to the mountains. After another day Jan Nio Oei's furlough was also up, and she returned to her job at the hospital.War and medicine have a way of occupying one's mind. Both Henk in the mountains and Jan in the hospital forgot each other. Henk got involved with the wash maid in his camp—a Sundanese girl, from the western part of the island of Java, who seemed to have been involved with every soldier in the camp at one time or another.

Jan Nio Oei proceeded to find a boyfriend in Semarang, the Dutch private assigned to chauffeur the nurses on their rounds. Jan's father was as protective as ever: when Jan went out to see her boyfriend, her father sent Jan's little sister, Tjoei, along for safekeeping. But Jan found that her sister was always happy to go away for a nickel.

Then one day, months later, in August of 1949, Jan ran across the slip of paper with Henk's name and address on it. In a single moment the embarrassment of the final non-encounter, there in front of the camera shop, recurred in her mind, and she sat down to write her mystery soldier and play a little game with him.

"Dear Mijnheer Henk,

"It has been so long since we met here in Semarang..."

Jan draped each sentence in just enough fluttering femininity to draw him in—designing her words to make herself sound interested in him, but carefully constructing each phrase to avoid an outright lie.

Henk rarely got mail of any kind. This letter left him puzzled. He remembered the girl named Jan from the camera shop—but this letter came from Bodjong Hospital, signed by nurse Jan, and Henk could not remember messing around with any nurses in Semarang. She had carefully withheld her last name and home address, telling just enough to play the game: she was nineteen, a Catholic, et cetera, et cetera...

Henk sat in his rough room in the jungle town of Karangpandang and studied the letter. It had done its job—he was drawn in, flattered and intrigued. But to write back would take true diplomatic aplomb, and the novelist's sense of suspense.

First, he decided, a dash of dark glamour:

"Dear Jan,

"I received your letter this afternoon, and I am writing back while I work the night watch, guarding against guerrilla attacks here in our jungle outpost."

Now perhaps some syrup, and a pinch of self-pity:

"I have waited so long to hear from you. I thought perhaps you had forgotten about me already."

Then, backing off, some news-as-usual material:

"Soon the towns of Kalisoro and Tawangmangoe here in our area will be given their freedom and turned over to the TNI."

Then, taking the plunge, risking a mistake and pretending to be sure that this nurse Jan was the same camera-shop Jan that he had met months earlier:

"I think back to May, when I had leave, and I went to Semarang to see my brother, John, off to Holland, and where I had my first encounter with you in the photography shop, and later chatted with you on the way home."

Henk took a deep breath and kept writing. He was in over his head now; he would have to swim for the opposite shore:

"I want to explain to you in this letter that the reason I wanted to make your acquaintance was because you seemed friendly and helpful in the camera shop, and when I saw you there I immediately wanted to strike up a conversation with you. I want you to know that I am interested in you as a person and not in something else."

Henk looked at his own writing, wondering about the tone. Maybe it sounded a little too apologetic? He would counter with a line or two of Great White Hero:

"At least meeting you in Semarang was a refreshing change in my constant routine, such as it is, with all the fighting in the villages, and the constant threat of death I meet with every day."

Or perhaps he shouldn't be too harsh. Maybe this distant pen pal would like to see a more tender side. Henk decided to test those waters next with a couple lines:

"Out here in the thick of the battle, you sometimes wish for someone to love, instead of always having to fight and hate. They say soldiers are rough, but in their hearts they aren't."

Now it was time for a little flattery:

"Since that day I met you, I have thought a lot of you."

Henk reread the line, then added a sentence:

"Even though I don't know your last name."

Finally Henk's curiosity got the better of him. He decided to ask directly:

"Are you the same Jan I met at the camera shop? You called yourself nurse Jan on the envelope, but I didn't think you were a nurse. How did you get my address? Certainly you were the only Jan I met in Semarang, and the only girl I got acquainted with at all in that town."

Henk decided to go for broke:

"Write me back right away. I don't get any mail from anyone—and, by the way, I don't have a girlfriend in Holland."

Then, afraid of scaring off his only potential pen pal, he eased off once again.

"Getting married is something I don't foresee for my immediate future, so don't let that notion be a burden to you."

With a few more lines of amiable chitchat, Henk wrapped up the letter—closing with "A handshake from me and Eddie," his ragamuffin camp dog—and hurriedly mailed it off.

Jan read the quick response with a sly grin. Her Dutch soldier-boy had danced the very dance she wanted to see. This could be interesting. She would write him again. It might be amusing to see how long this Dutchman could do the emotional pirouette.

5

Chance Reunion

Henk's duties slipped and shifted as the war degenerated for the Dutch. Where once he had led the fight against Sukarno's guerrilla forces, striving to crush them, now he was fighting just to keep from being crushed. In town after town, the guerrillas gained ground, until finally the Dutch government sent down the directive to begin turning territory over to the hated Sukarno and the forces of the TNI.

Henk looked around him at the once beautiful land of Indonesia. It sickened him, as war-torn Holland had sickened him. Kalisoro, one of Indonesia's loveliest resort areas, lay in ruins. Expensive homes stood fire-blackened, empty shells gutted by the maniacal fighting, their swimming pools and tennis courts mangled by bombings and automatic rifle fire. Kalisoro had been stripped of its electricity. There was no running water in the city. And now, in the aftermath, Holland was turning Kalisoro over to the rebels. Henk shook his head. What was it worth to them now?

In Kalisoro, as in so many other towns, Henk found himself in charge of turning over the corpse of the place to the TNI. In the strange passion of the Indonesian conflict, fighting was still going on all around, even as the Dutch relinquished sector after sector of the island chain. Henk and his men, then, were fighting the hands they were feeding—trying to give land to the rebels without letting the rebels kill them. It was tense, gritty, ugly work, staking out a hopefully secure bunker of clearing and establishing unofficial lines of communication with the area's guerrillas, negotiating by day and standing guard by night. And still, for hundreds and thousands of Indonesians, even with their homes and communities lying razed around them, life went on.

There was a certain status quo even in war. The camp personnel, roving from town to town like hopeless nomads, stayed essentially the same, even down to the hangers-on, like the Sundanese wash maid who still had an unresolved liking for Henk. The whole ragtag operation tramped through the war together.

Jan's next letter followed Henk to Kalisoro, and in it she playfully suggested that she might visit him there in a few weeks. Henk was eager, but he dutifully wrote her back and advised her that nobody was vacationing there any more. Still, he wanted to see her—slipping deeper into her web—and he told her to come ahead, and as quickly as she could. At least, he thought, they could be together—and perhaps entertain themselves playing makeshift volleyball on a blackened patch of earth like the rest of the soldiers did.

Again Jan was amused by the speedy reply, but less wickedly. The guy obviously cared about her, gravitating to the only affection he may have experienced in years, and she found it hard to separate herself from that. Her own boyfriend had no idea she was carrying on the correspondence—it didn't start as something she intended to last for long—but she could detect in herself a slight and growing interest in this Henk.

She wrote him again, with less guile. He had mentioned that his term in the Dutch army would soon be up, and now she wanted to know his plans. She also remembered him mentioning his birthday, and now she realized it was approaching. She sent a card, wished him a happy birthday, and asked if he had received birthday greetings from his family in Holland.

The birthday card caught up with Henk in the hospital in Tasikmadoe. He had contracted a painful ear infection in Kalisoro, and it had put him on his back for a few days. The card caught him off guard. Her questions poked through his misty memory—and it was uncomfortable.

"Yesterday I received your letter wishing me a happy birthday," he wrote, his emotions a little mixed. "I was very happy with it—it was the first birthday card I ever received. I hadn't even remembered it was my birthday..."

"You asked me if I received birthday wishes from my relatives at home. I have none, only my older brother."

"When you ask me a question like that, it often brings up the old memories of my parents..."

"You also say in a year I'll be back in Holland. But that would be a difficult move for me, because of the past. That was the reason I left Holland and joined the service—to leave the ugly past behind..."

Henk liked the prospect of returning to Holland less and less. He began putting out lines to various segments of the Dutch military bureaucracy, trying to locate a position that would leave him in Indonesia, even though many Dutch were being evacuated as tensions increased throughout the country. He wanted to stay—to avoid facing Holland again, and to stay at least in reasonably close touch with his intriguing nurse in Semarang.

Meanwhile Jan was growing closer and closer to her Dutch chauffeur-boyfriend, close proximity winning the love-war. And Henk's letters became—simultaneously—more commonplace and more of an oddity. Her responses to him grew more sporadic, lapsing sometimes for weeks, and at one point even for months. Henk thoroughly hooked, always quizzed her paranoically.

"Did I say something to offend you? Are there other soldiers there in Semarang? What is the problem?"

But Jan always soothed him short of complete panic by making a pleasant suggestion about getting together sometime in the future. She could never bring herself to cut him off.

As 1949 slipped toward 1950, Henk grabbed a military librarian's job and had his term extended to October. But he was restless. He wanted to know more about this girl he felt so strangely attracted to—and yet really knew little of.

So he decided to surprise her, with a visit.

━━━

Sukarno's forces had gained strength and were soon to force the Dutch hand on the question of total independence. The Dutch army and the Knil were packing their bags fearfully. And the tensions seemed to draw each racial group into its own corner: the European Dutch opposite the Indonesian-born Dutch, the Indonesians opposite the Chinese, who in fact would soon be required to change to Indonesian names or be subjected to an annual tax. The old easy mix, the comfortable camaraderie, was gone. In its place was the angry edge of bigotry and distrust.

—*mm*—

The head nurse found Jan on her rounds and advised her that she had company in the lobby. Jan expected her chauffeur-boyfriend.

There was a moment of startled silence when she opened the door and faced Henk in his uniform, half-grinning at her. His pen pal, nurse Jan, was the same Jan from the photography shop he had met many months earlier.

Jan was sheepish, not entirely willing to be friendly after the year of intrigue.

"What are you doing here?" she asked a little too pointedly.

Henk explained that he was in the region on military business.

"May I take you to your home after work this evening?" he asked politely.

"I'm sorry; my dad is picking me up," Jan lied.

Henk let a short breath escape. He hadn't known what to expect, but somehow he hadn't expected this.

"All right, I'll...be going."

Deflated, troubled, Henk returned to his base and spilled out a long, tumultuous letter. When he had spent his emotions completely, he read the letter and then tore it to shreds. Then, calmer, he reduced the contents to a short, polite little letter that essentially left the door wide open to Jan.

Jan, meanwhile, rattled by the surprise visit, wrestled with feelings of guilt over the snubbing she had given her devoted pen pal. But her boyfriend—also Dutch, also a soldier—commanded her heart. When Henk's letter came, Jan struggled for a response. Could she keep corresponding with this persistent Henk, even when it was clear her boyfriend would soon ask her to marry him?

Finally Jan decided to show Henk's letter to her boyfriend and see what he would say.

Could she write him back, she asked her boyfriend, on a strictly friendly basis?

Boyfriend said no.

When Henk got no reply, he wrote again. Still no answer, but he wrote again. The Sundanese wash maid, still lurking in Henk's periphery, was irritated by his devotion; but he kept on writing. The wash maid was, after all, only a wash maid, and she meant nothing to him. Jan hung in his mind, like a pleasant painting.

―――

The Catholic chaplain was upset that one of his men would get so serious with a Buddhist-born Chinese nurse. But Jan and the chauffeur were definitely talking about marriage, and the problem had to be worked out.

She was practically already a Catholic, she explained to the chaplain. She had wanted to become a Christian since she was a little girl, she told him.

No, he insisted, she could not marry this soldier because she was not originally a Catholic. Besides, it was unhealthy in this day and age for a local girl to marry a Dutch serviceman. And

Jan's boyfriend, a serious young man with a deep sense of religious and civil responsibility, could not bring himself to buck the system. As a private, he probably had no chance of success anyway. It would take a special dispensation from his superiors.

The anger and frustration boiled up inside her as she faced the rigid military and religious machines. There were days of tears. Jan thought she would die with the grief. The situation was so unfair, so painful.

Then, suddenly, her chauffeur was gone—a different private showing up in the driver's seat one day. Her boyfriend had been shipped without warning to Holland in a major troop transfer. He wrote her faithfully, but hopelessly. He did not have the spunk to fight the bureaucracy for her.

Mr. and Mrs. Oei wagged their fingers at Jan as the story spilled out of her. You just can't trust those Dutch servicemen, they insisted.

Anxious, anguishing, alone, Jan took a few days off to travel to Bandung. Her Uncle Siong would put her up, and maybe she could get her emotional house back in order.

On his new job, Henk picked up a bug. The doctor identified it as yellow jaundice and prescribed a few weeks of rest in a pleasant climate. Henk was packed off to Bandung for R & R.

Day by day he grew stronger, and the yellow in his face was slowly restored to its usual ruddy Dutch pink. As the color returned, Henk rebuilt his strength by taking gradually longer walks downtown. He found himself thinking about Jan, but he refused to agonize.

He was gazing casually into a shop window when he saw her. She was inspecting merchandise intently. At first he thought it was his imagination and not really Jan at all. To run into her by sheer coincidence like this—in Bandung, where neither of them belonged—was more than he could believe for the first few seconds.

When she first looked up and saw him, she had no reaction. But spontaneously they smiled at each other and each moved toward the doorway.

"*Dag, Mijnheer,*" she offered tentatively in the traditional Dutch.

"*Dag, Mevrouw,*" he replied in the same tone. Then, after a moment's hesitation: "Would you like to get lunch?"

"Yes."

They began walking. There was a café only a few doors away.

"You haven't written in a long time," he suggested as carefully as he could.

"I know. I've had some problems."

He waited.

"I was going to get married."

His eyebrows moved up for a moment, then settled back. As she confessed the events of the past months, his face softened. He had been had—and yet, she was charming.

She finished talking and sighed deeply. She felt dirty, wasted.

"Why didn't you come to me?" Henk asked quietly. "I could have helped you."

She looked up at him. It was a surprising response.

"Yes?" she asked quizzically.

"I have rank on that chaplain. I could have worked things out for you and your private."

She was unable to accept the notion.

"You would have helped me?"

"Of course," Henk answered, smiling. "I don't like to hear you being unhappy."

Jan looked into his eyes. There were no lies there.

They sat for hours in the café, talking through the endless detail of two convergent pasts. They laughed and nodded and shook their heads and drank tea in quantity. Somewhere in the meandering conversation, she told him of her childhood dreams and hopes, of the man hanging on the cross, of her longing to become a Christian—and he responded supportively. He told her of his months of aching loneliness in Holland, the long nights in the underground, of his bitterness—and she responded soothingly.

Each had found a remote quality of softness in the other.

Yes, she would like to see him again tomorrow. But perhaps it would be better if she got herself to Uncle Siong's place alone. Henk's blond hair would not go over well there, especially right now. Her family was less favorably disposed toward Dutch servicemen now than usually.

They were together the entire enchanting week, in cafés, at movies, walking and window-shopping—and before it ended, Henk had asked her to marry him. They could be married by a Dutch Reformed chaplain—Henk could work it out—even though, with the trouble between the Dutch and the

Indonesians, interracial marriage was the last thing the military wanted to deal with at the moment.

Jan, still smarting over the chauffeur, hesitated. She told Henk she would marry him, but inside she wasn't sure. She would rather think about it awhile. She wondered if she could truly, truly trust this Dutchman.

Still, she was fascinated. Here was the opportunity she had longed for: a Christian home. For even though Henk was not a Catholic, according to her only knowledge of Christians, still he was European. And Jan knew that all Europeans were Christians. It was common knowledge, wasn't it?

6

Tug-of-War

The train ride back to Semarang from Bandung was twelve tough hours long, and when Jan got home she fell into a deep sleep. In the middle of the night she found herself walking along an unfamiliar street. As she walked, a woman approached her, floating on a bed which came to a stop in front of her, blocking her in the road. The woman, obviously European, was gray-headed, with one eye clear and the other eye cloudy. She sat up in the bed and looked directly at Jan.

"Go with Henk wherever he goes," she said in Dutch. "Follow him."

The woman lay back down, and the strange floating bed drifted away and out of sight. Jan began to walk again, and after a long time she came upon an isolated square of land. She stood on the square and looked forward into the distance. Far away she could see a mountain of muck and filth, and on the mountain a building bathed in beautiful light. She could just barely make out the figure of a man—was it Henk?—scrambling and clawing up the side of the mountain, trying to reach that beautiful building. Yes, it was Henk; but he couldn't quite reach the goal.

Jan blinked and awoke, startled. She ran the dream over and over in her mind. What did it mean? Who was the Dutch woman with the cloudy eye? Where was Henk going? The questions crowded her head until her mind whirled.

Somehow, she just couldn't be sure about marrying this man.

Henk, meanwhile, had no idea that his lovely Chinese bride-to-be had any reservations at all. And Henk never looked back.

When the Sundanese wash maid heard him say that he was going to marry, she flew into a rage. But Henk could not consider it seriously. It was a schoolgirl crush, nothing more.

Still on medical leave in Bandung, he plunged into the paperwork and planning that the complex interracial situation would require.

It was the worst of all possible worlds. For a Dutch service-man to marry a native Indonesian against the backdrop of 1950 would be a delicate and difficult achievement. The military bureaucracy, straining to maintain equilibrium in an increasingly hostile environment, reacted to Henk's application for a marriage license. The Dutch government required evidence in such cases that the bride-to-be was not a prostitute or indigent, and there were reams of paperwork to be signed and counter-signed by dozens of officials in various locations and positions. For one thing, Jan would have to get the mayor of her home-town and another acquaintance to certify her good health and good standing in the community. The court would also have to stamp its approval. It would take some time. Henk's legal guardian back in Holland, Oom Theo, a longtime friend of the Rijfkogel family, had to be consulted and his approval registered in military files. Furthermore, Chinese custom would require the blessing of the Oei family—something far more difficult than Jan had indicated to Henk it would be.

Henk pounced on the multiple obstacles and began wrestling them enthusiastically to the ground. Within a day of Jan's departure for Semarang, he had mailed off a letter to her, reporting that he had begun the process of getting his birth certificate and other papers from Holland and all the necessary forms from the Dutch military in Jakarta. He hurried on to tell her that he wanted to come as soon as possible to Semarang to meet her parents. He thought he might be able to fly in—even though such a flight was by now prohibited for Dutch servicemen, Henk had his good Indonesian captain friend who could pull a few strings.

Jan was horrified. She had not yet told her parents about this sudden change of life plan, and she certainly had no intention of working up the nerve to do so very soon. She had not even convinced herself that marrying this boy was a good idea.

Henk's letter went on to say that he was working on getting a Dutch Reformed chaplain to perform the ceremony—but things were already difficult, because of the political tension, and bound to get more difficult yet. Sukarno was demanding complete and absolute evacuation by the Dutch, and Dutch corpses were becoming more and more common discoveries in alleys and rivers and abandoned buildings.

"So hurry," Henk wrote, "and send your papers to the Semarang city government office. Make sure, too, that you put down on all your papers that you are a nurse. And be sure to communicate all of this to your parents."

Enclosed in the same envelope was another letter, this one written directly to Mr. and Mrs. Oei. Jan read it, wide eyed:

"Although I know we are strangers, I am fond of you already. I very much want to meet you and express my thankfulness for taking me as your son-in-law…"

Jan folded the letter back up and swallowed hard. Her parents would not see this.

And yet she was too fond of Henk to stop him cold. The next day she sent him cuff links for his birthday—"They brought tears to my eyes," he wrote effusively the following week—and she said nothing in her letters about her parents.

She also stalled on her paperwork. Her believable excuse was the war's upheaval of Semarang. City government was at a virtual standstill as the Sukarno rebellion hurled through the Semarang region like a Pacific hurricane. Soon it would be off-limits to all Dutch.

Henk was his own Pacific hurricane. He wrote back to suggest they marry elsewhere. He also reported that Jan would need to write Oom Theo herself, asking permission to marry Henk.

"Have you communicated all of this to your parents?" he asked in the last line of the letter.

Jan read it and sighed.

She decided to wade out a bit into the storm and express some of her feelings. But she was too timid. Henk misunderstood, and thought she was worried about being able to get approval for the wedding. He answered a little irritably.

"You're just all shook up, and down in the mouth because of all the chaos. It hasn't been too easy for me, either, you know, living in all this uncertainty. Just be calm."

And Henk was marching on. He reported that he had visited Jakarta's Sociale Dienst, the social services bureau where his paperwork could either be facilitated or forgotten. There were some difficulties, but he was wringing out the results manually. It was especially difficult in part because he did not have Jan's parents' permission in hand yet. Could she hurry?

"And I will do my best," he assured her, "to get to you there in Semarang, even though it is closed off to me."

Henk's passion for the great task was unyielding, unquenchable. He kept working the dominee, the minister of the Dutch Reformed Church, urging him in letter after letter to agree to marry them, and quickly. With each uneasy letter from Jan, Henk shot back a corrective epistle, either stern or buoyant in tone, depending on what he sensed she needed to hear.

"Fear not," he went so far as to write in one impassioned letter. "God is with you." He was willing to shoot all the guns to win this personal war.

Henk was considering, too, in his quieter moments, the abandoned God his fiancée longed to serve. Sometimes it seemed that perhaps God was a living being after all, and that He might even care about the course of a human destiny. But usually...

—————

Jan was still fidgeting inside, anxious and uncertain. Then one day, out of one of the many envelopes she received from Henk, she pulled a photograph. Henk had sent her a prized snapshot of his lost family—one of the photographs from the roll of film that had been retrieved from the Rhine so long before. On the left side, Henk's handwritten caption explained, was his sister Boukje. On the right was one of Boukje's friends. In the middle, he wrote, was his dear mother.

Jan's gaze locked in on the middle face, her eyes riveted to the eyes looking back at her. One of the woman's eyes was clear; the other eye was cloudy.

A shiver ran the course of Jan's body. She had never seen a picture of Henk's mother before. But this, undeniably, was the European woman she had seen in her puzzling dream weeks earlier.

"Go with Henk," she could recall the figure saying to her, "where he goes. Follow him."

Jan felt the jelly shaping up and solidifying inside her, the old indecision giving way to a new resolve. She knew this was her man, her partner for life. No matter whether dreams were to be trusted. That was a theoretical question. As for Jan Nio Oei, she had been given her mandate. It was enough for her.

She would marry this Dutch serviceman. She could worry about how to tell her parents later on.

In her heart she was gleeful. She would finally have her Christianity—a Christian home with this European soldier.

Unless something went wrong.

In the hourglass of 1949, time slipped by with greater and greater speed. Events tumbled over one another until it seemed that suddenly one day Indonesia was given her independence by Holland. The celebration rocked the islands as thousands shouted "Merdeka! Freedom!" in national union.

Evacuation was swift. Dutch people—from the transient soldiers to the tenth-generation Knil—crated their belongings and prepared to ship themselves out. Some were merely sad, others swollen with fury. But none could deny the tidal wave of Indonesian sentiment that Sukarno had generated so skillfully; the Dutch, stripped of their power and no longer considered necessary, must exit.

Of course there were the inevitable remnant: a handful of military and economic advisers, an agricultural expert or two. Henk, in fact, was put in charge of the transfer of ammunition and supplies to the Indonesians, and in that role he was still on Indonesian soil when the last of his colleagues had shipped out. He would work through the last of his assignments—a few months' worth of work, perhaps—and then...?

Henk didn't care if the whole population sailed for Europe as Merdeka came to Indonesia, as long as his marriage license application went through.

Merdeka, however, had changed the rules substantially. At every turn there was a new obstacle. When the dominee suddenly fled Indonesia, leaving Henk without the marrying minister he had so meticulously cultivated, the young Dutchman felt the weariness more than ever before.

"I sometimes feel," he wrote on the sixth anniversary of his mother's death, "that I can ask God to help us. But the next time I could curse Him, because of the way things are going."

"And I wonder what you really think of my beliefs about God, whether you can accept the way I feel about that, and accept me with all your heart and soul."

"With all these paperwork problems, plus the events of my past," Henk wrote two days later, "it's hard for me to believe in

God, or to believe that He loves me and cares about me. If He did, He wouldn't have the both of us living in such uncertainty."

But Henk was wavering. His letter continued:

"Or should we learn to ask Him to help us and let Him lead us? Is He trying to make me bow down before Him so that later on He can make everything all right?"

"I always think I can do everything by myself—please don't think badly of me, Jan, because of the way I am. It's hard for me to be broken and bow down. Please help me, Jan, to learn this."

And then, the same closing question once again: "What is your family saying about all our plans?"

Jan's family was saying nothing. They had still not yet been told. Jan had determined to marry Henk, but she had still not been able to work up the nerve to confront her parents with the decision. Fearing their reaction, she was paralyzed, unable to move ahead on her paperwork, unable to tell Henk that she had not yet talked to them.

Henk, continuing his crusade, wrangled yet another extension on his term. He was growing more and more concerned about the problems Jan kept telling him she was facing. And he was still facing problems on his own end.

When his birth certificate finally arrived from Holland, Henk went to his captain with it for the single signature his papers required under Dutch military law.

"But you can't marry an Indonesian *now*," the captain whined. "The government of Holland can't guarantee your safety now as it is. How do you think we're going to protect you if you marry a native?"

Henk's face grew red and hot. His view of the world had soured because of stuff like this. His father, helpless, had died in the hands of Germany, a vile nation. The Allies had taken his mother and sister. Now Holland and Indonesia were playing tug-of-war with his fiancée.

"Look," he responded hotly, "I'm going to marry this girl one way or the other. If the Dutch won't authorize it, I'll relinquish my citizenship and join the Indonesian army."

The captain was jolted. "Oh come now."

"I'm serious," Henk shot back. "I've had my offers." He thought about his friend, the Indonesian captain who had challenged Henk to shoot him years before. The captain had often invited Henk to join him in the Indonesian military.

"I'm sick of red tape and paperwork and delays," Henk continued. "I've had my fill of countries arm wrestling and breaking people in the process. This is not politics anymore. This is my life, and Jan's life. And we are going to be married. You just tell me what country you want me to be fighting for when I'm done."

The captain shook his head and sighed.

"You're a good soldier. We should lose the Indonesian people in this mess, not the Dutch."

He bent over the desk, signed the paper, and handed it to Henk. Henk turned around and marched away. Finally, perhaps, the people had won one over the governments.

Now the only hurdle was Jan's package of documents, papers she was presumably wading through in Semarang. Each time she wrote she described the latest accomplishments—and hassles. But the mail moved slowly, and Henk was never satisfied by knowing where things stood so many days after the fact.

Frustrated, Henk decided to take leave, risk discipline, and go to Semarang in person.

7

A Kitchen Too Hot

He could only get seventy-two-hour leave. The Indonesian captain promised to arrange a flight for him, but even the captain could not control events in the whirlwind of Merdeka, and the plan fell through. To boat across to Semarang would take more time than Henk had available. The only alternative was the train.

By now, in the tension of Merdeka, the train was off-limits to all Dutch. It was considered dangerous for a white-skinned person to travel on public transportation with some four hundred Indonesians—whites had been known to disappear between cities, their corpses sometimes turning up in sad shape, sometimes not turning up at all. Rioting was common as rowdy Dutchmen sometimes taunted gloating Indonesians—and vice versa—on the long train rides.

Henk spent very little time making up his mind. He got on the train, brash and bold, just waiting for someone to challenge him. Nobody did.

He found his way to Jan's house, eventually walking the old route along which he had trailed her that first day more than two years before. As he walked, he stopped occasionally to ask directions, referring to an old letter that mentioned her home address. At about eight p.m., he was knocking on the door.

Jan's mother appeared in the doorway.

"Is Jan here?"

The woman's face clouded over. She did not speak Dutch, but she heard her daughter's name. She disappeared into the house. In a moment Jan came to the door, her hand touching her throat as if to say, "The jig is up."

"What are you doing here?" she asked by reflex.

"I—what does that mean?" Henk replied. "May I come in?"

Jan's eyes were wide and worried.

"I never told them."

"What?" There was a trace of screech in his voice.

"Come in, we'll see how it goes."

And she hustled him into the living room.

Tea was brought out in due course and offered all around. Jan's father, like a tremendous Buddhist statue, sat silent and sullen, his eyes locked on the Dutch boy's pale face. Henk and Mrs. Oei squeezed out a little conversation, with Jan guardedly translating from Indonesian to Dutch and back again.

"Why didn't you tell us, dear?"

"I didn't know he was coming today, Mother."

"Why didn't you tell them, Jan?"

"I didn't know how, Henk. Just keep smiling."

"But when will you get married, dear?"

"What is she saying, Jan?"

"She says you're a fine-looking young man."

"I don't know when we're getting married, Mother. I haven't got our papers together."

"Do you have all the papers together yet, Jan?"

"What is he saying, Jan?"

"He's saying what a lovely home you have here, Mother."

"Henk, we need to talk about the papers."

"Aren't you going to marry me, Jan?"

"Yes, I'm going to marry you. I just haven't been able to get the papers."

"Does this mean you will be married Christian, dear?"

"Well, Jan, our dominee shipped out a couple weeks ago, and the chaplain has gone too. So we have nobody left to marry us in a Christian ceremony like you wanted."

"Mother, I think it should be up to Father how I'm married."

"I have nothing to do with a Dutch soldier marrying a daughter of mine."

"What did he say, Jan?"

"He said he hopes you treat me kindly all the days of your life."

"Well, of course I will. I promised I would in my letter to them."

"What is he saying to your father, dear?"

"He says he is sorry if he has offended our household in any way."

"He certainly has."

"Father says you are most kind, Henk."

The anxious encounter was cut short. Jan's father excused himself to his own room, followed obediently by Mrs. Oei—the customary Chinese signal of disapproval. Jan and Henk were left in the front room. Henk's insecurities burst forth in angry questions. What was she trying to prove, stringing out the legal process? Did she want to get married—or was she playing with him again, like she did in the beginning? He was hurt, and frightened.

Jan's insecurities came out in tearful answers. She had been frightened, and with no one to consult she had followed her instincts. She was sorry.

They talked for hours, until their bumpy emotions had smoothed out. Jan promised to get the papers together immediately. Henk kissed her warmly and headed for the local barracks, where the Indonesian captain had arranged safe lodging for him.

Back inside, Jan cornered her mother and poured out her heart. She told her about the first meeting with Henk, the chance reunion in Bandung, the dream about Henk's mother. Desperately she exposed her old inner longing—to have a Christian home. Her mother listened motionless, until she was done, then nodded with a slight Chinese smile.

"If you truly love him," she said, "perhaps we can work things out. But there's so much trouble with the Dutch right now."

"I know, Mother. But we love each other."

"I understand how you feel. Of course we don't agree with you. But I'll talk to your father."

It turned out to be a futile exercise. Jan's father would not talk. His mind had already shut like a clamp on the subject.

He never spoke to his daughter again.

Jan's mother, having pledged her help to Jan, followed Chinese protocol and discussed the matter with the oldest other male member of the family, her own brother. Together they decided Jan was to be married in a Buddhist temple.

When the last of the paperwork had been assembled, including Mrs. Oei's signature of approval, the only missing element turned out to be Jan's signature on a few papers. She would have to come to Bandung, where Henk was still stationed, even though it was very dangerous for her to travel into the region. Henk hit upon a daring plan. He arranged with a friend, Lieutenant Prachman, to let Jan pose as the lieutenant's wife. Military wives could be exempted from some restrictions, and the ruse would make travel safer for Jan. Prachman would send her a telegram, addressed to his wife, instructing her to take a flight from Semarang to Bandung. The train between the two cities was legal for Jan, but the rail system had become so dangerous and service so sporadic that Henk decided the illegal air flight would be safer. Jan was to take Prachman's telegram to the Basis Comando, posing as Mrs. Prachman, and get on the plane.

"Don't be afraid," Henk wrote her. "The train ride is much worse."

The telegram failed to arrive. Something had gone wrong. Henk, fidgeting and feeling the pressure, sent the paperwork to Semarang by way of a risky messenger.

But the final signatures were applied to the final forms, and finally, the wedding date was set.

━━━

The ceremony was strange for Henk. Christian weddings had always been strange enough for him—odd, uncomfortable little slices of time, when emotions seemed to taunt the will. The Buddhist procedure, moreover, bore only a remote connection to the Christian format. This coming together of the Eastern world and the Western world was disorienting for him.

Maybe after it was all over, he thought—when the whole ordeal had ended—things would settle down to some semblance of normal.

He thought wrong.

━━━

There was a total of two weeks of bliss in the Rijfkogel marriage. They spent their first two weeks honeymooning in Semarang. In romantic moments, Henk promised to take her to Holland to visit— someday. With Jan by his side, the past might not seem quite as hostile. But that, he told himself, was far in the future.

Then they headed to Jakarta, for Henk to continue his work and Jan to settle into life as a serviceman's wife.

But a telegram was waiting for them when they arrived. It was an official communication from the Dutch government.

The international kitchen had gotten too hot. All Dutch military personnel were to send their wives and children home to Holland immediately "for their own security." Servicemen could follow as soon as their specific projects were concluded.

Henk was flabbergasted. The order could put Jan alone in Holland for months while he finished his inventory project. Jan was terrified. Sitting in their little apartment, they talked in circles until the small hours of the morning. There were so few options.

Henk went in to his superior officer and slapped the telegram on his desk.

"She was to stay here," he argued angrily. "She has no family in Europe. She's never been outside of Indonesia in her life."

"Your lives aren't safe," the officer answered matter-of-factly. "She can't stay."

"Then I can't stay," Henk replied. "I won't send her alone."

They argued for several minutes. Finally the harried officer sighed.

"I'll see what I can do."

For nearly two weeks the bureaucracy shuffled through interminable questions and nonanswers. Then, suddenly, only a month after their wedding, Henk and Jan walked up the gangway onto the Dutch oceanliner that would carry them to Holland. In the whirlwind of packing and farewell bidding, neither of them had a chance to consider the tragedy. With no telephones and a slow postal service, Jan's parents could not be contacted.

As the ship made its way west, Jan cried in the evenings, the jolting exodus overwhelming her. She could not bring herself to sit down and write her parents. She could not even give them an address in Holland; they had no idea where they would be stationed once they arrived.

Henk was sullen. He had never wanted to live in Holland again. He would have been content to spend the rest of his life in Indonesia. Even if he were forced to leave, he had often mused, he would go to Korea or somewhere else in the Pacific where the Dutch presence was allowed. But never back to re-live the trauma that was Europe.

The anger seeped into each of their spirits. Life had forced them to take a ride. And for Henk, it was just another in a long series of unhappy rides. Jan, he had thought, might signal a fresh beginning for him. But now even this—after conquering so much conflict to get married—had soured on him.

He leaned on the railing, staring out blankly at the horizon. As the ship steamed toward Holland, Henk spit into the Atlantic.

PART II:

SECRET WARS

8

The Flower

They docked in Amsterdam on the twenty-fourth day. Jan had only a single suitcase of summer clothing. Henk had only a gunnysack with his clothes and his government-issued footlocker. He had shipped his big trunk, full of souvenirs and junk, to his legal guardian Oom Theo—in Huissen, near the site of the bombing that had killed Henk's mother—until he could find a place to store the huge thing.

It was a new world for both of them. The land that Henk had erased from his memory now surrounded him, with all its old sameness made new by the passage of time—and all its newness besides. For Jan, Holland was the ultimate fantasy. She had never seen snow or felt its accompanying temperatures. She had never seen modern housing of the continental variety. Telephones were mysterious. Only the language was familiar.

The army installed them immediately in a small eight-unit apartment compound in the remote woody bossen of Kootwijk. Some quarter-of-a-million Dutch had fled Indonesia, and the thousands who were military had to be placed wherever the government could find the space. For many of them—no matter how blond or blue-eyed—Holland had not been home for their families for hundreds of years. They were as lost as Jan.

The apartment was a single room, twelve by nine feet, which variously served as living room, bedroom, bathroom, kitchen, and laundromat. Jan unpacked her suitcase and put it into the tiny closet. Henk unpacked his gunnysack and slid his footlocker under the bed. They went out to buy Jan some winter clothes.

Life did not wait for the displaced couple to make many further adjustments. Henk went to work at Amersfoort, miles away, teaching younger Dutch soldiers to fend for themselves as he had against guerrillas. He dug in—albeit bitterly—to climb the Royal Dutch Army's ladder of success. Jan met her neighbors and set up housekeeping. One of the other wives in the little building helped her learn to sew.

Jan asked her neighbors about Christian churches in the area. The closest one was ten miles away. They had no car. Henk's schedule soon brought him home at odd hours. He usually came home tired.

Soon Jan was pregnant. The quest for a Christian home faded from her mind.

When Johanna was born, she revolutionized the household in a baby's usual way. The little Dutch cradle now became the center of attention. The apartment filled with milk and diapers and toys.

But eventually the routine was established, and in her quiet moments Jan looked at her baby and thought back to her own childhood...to that crucified figure...and the old longing returned.

A Catholic priest, a chaplain, appeared at the door one morning, making his rounds of the Dutch military people. He asked the usual questions and heard Jan explain her confusion. She had thought she was Catholic in Indonesia, until the Catholic chaplain there had told her no. Then she thought she had become a Protestant by marrying Henk—but now apparently that was not true either, because she had failed to attend church anywhere. The priest assured her she was welcome at the Catholic church; he offered to baptize Johanna right there in the apartment. Later, when Jan told Henk, he was furious. The Catholics had given them the runaround in Indonesia—now they were circling like vultures. Jan did not pursue it.

Days later, a Protestant minister called in similar style and invited the Rijfkogels to his church.

Henk shrugged off Jan's suggestions about attending church. Neither the Catholics nor the Protestants interested him. Church was too far away, too inconvenient. And he saw the good chances for acceleration in the military. He was busy.

Jan concealed her hurt. She knew Henk had a lot of bitterness inside. God had not rescued Henk's father nor spared his mother and sister. Maybe, she thought, after a little more time here in Holland, a little more time in her care, he would come around.

A grimy peddler showed up on the doorstep shortly thereafter. A horrible stench preceded him. His face lit up when he saw the baby, now two months old. With a beautiful wrinkly smile, he laid her gently against his filthy shoulder. Jan was silently horrified. The baby was absolutely spotless at all times. The old man softly patted the infant's back and sighed.

"Has she been baptized?" he asked.

Jan was surprised by the question. "Well, no," she answered hesitantly.

"Ah…this child needs to be baptized," the old man said, closing his eyes and swaying lightly with the baby.

Something clicked inside of Jan in that moment. When Henk came home, she bombarded him. When were they going to have the Christian home he had promised her since Bandung?

He didn't want to talk about it.

⸻

Things deteriorated. These two people did not understand much about each other. The tension grew and—more and more often—snapped.

Arguments over church occurred week by week, eventually giving way to other issues as well. Jan thought Henk was too friendly with the lady who helped people on and off the public trolley. Henk thought she was being silly, and said so—loudly. Jan responded by dredging up his past dalliances, real and imagined. That Sundanese wash maid was a good case in point! She had seen a stray picture of her in his scrapbook.

There were good times, but only as punctuation marks.

Every day saw a clash. Tiny problems started major skirmishes. Tempers flared more easily with every incident. One afternoon Henk was sitting on the bed, pulling on his boots, getting ready to leave for the night shift. They were arguing. Jan was livid. Suddenly she lunged at him and sank her teeth into his arm. When he pulled away, she had his stripes clenched between her teeth, and there was a wide rip in the shirtsleeve of his uniform. Henk slapped her across the face. She spat the stripes back at him. The battle raged on.

No one knew about the conflict. Henk was too embarrassed to mention it to any officers. Jan was too confused to feel comfortable discussing it with other wives in the compound. Henk never wrote his brother or Oom Theo about it; Jan never wrote her mother about it. To the outside world, it was a happy, healthy marriage. The war was self-contained.

And neither of the warring parties knew exactly why it was all happening.

Henk was reassigned. The new position brought him home only one day a week. The war at home was forced to cool off.

Now Jan spent day after day in the cubicle alone. Her eyes took in every detail of the tiny room: the irregularities in the wall, the design flaws in the little vanity, the little military foot-locker under the bed...

It was the footlocker that her eyes kept coming back to. Somehow she began to feel distinctly that there was something unusual in that little box. She sat and frowned at it for long minutes at a time. Occasionally she would get up and move toward it; sometimes she even got down on her knees and began to pull it out from under the bed. But each time, she was stopped short, gripped by a paralyzing jolt—fear.

The box slowly took on a life of its own, commanding Jan's thoughts. As she lay in bed, she could not stop seeing it beneath her in her mind's eye. Sleep came with difficulty. Eventually she began having nightmares. She awoke choking and gasping for breath. Night after night she struggled to keep the box out of her thoughts. But all day she sat and stared at it, and at night it would not leave her alone.

She began to fear it would drive her mad.

Finally one day when Henk was home, she asked him what was in the footlocker.

"Oh, nothing," he shrugged. "Papers and things from Indonesia."

"Show me."

"Why bother? It's nothing."

"Please open it," she said with begging eyes.

Henk shook his head slightly, bent down, and slid the box out from under the bed. On his knees he opened it up and began naming each item nonchalantly. Documents were tightly banded together—their long-sought marriage papers included. Odd loose keys and other trivia cluttered the box. Henk took each thing out and replaced it casually.

Jan's eyes went directly to a tiny silver vase with a metal flower in it. It was darkened by years of tarnish.

"This was from that crazy little wash maid in our camp back in the mountains," Henk said as he plucked it out of the recesses of the box.

"It's been bothering me," Jan said, frowning.

"What do you mean, bothering you? You asked me what was in here."

"Something in this box has been bothering me," she repeated. "I know this is what it was. She put something on that flower to hurt me."

"Oh come on—"

"It happens," Jan insisted grimly. "It happens all the time in Indonesia. It's leyak. It's black magic. Please, Henk—throw it out."

He knew she could very well be right, but he resisted. "It's a good souvenir! It will be a keepsake someday!"

"Please. It will haunt me until you throw it away."

Henk smirked and raised his eyebrows sarcastically. He took the metal vase and flower and walked out the door.

The apartment was across from a small pond. Henk reared back and hurled the metal piece. It arced over the property and dropped in the pond with a *blup*.

Jan closed her eyes and exhaled slowly. Maybe now this tension would evaporate.

But the next day Henk left for duty, and Jan stood in the doorway looking at the surface of the pond. It was a pretty little place, a favorite walking spot for couples in the building. But as night fell again, Jan seemed to look through the glassy surface into the water. She could almost see that little flower coming to life, writhing and squirming to get out of that vase, striving to get up to the surface, struggling to get out and seek revenge on Jan for banishing her. Each night Jan grew more frightened, less rational—at the same time drawn to the pond and terrified of its hidden treasure. Night after night the dual magnetism grew more compelling, until finally Jan flung open the door and ran for the water's edge.

She looked into the pond, but she could see nothing. She searched all around the edges for a glimpse of the flower, pacing in the soft earth that encircled the little pond, peering into the water for even the slightest evidence of motion. But her darting eyes caught no movement. Suddenly she ran back to the house breathing spastically and near tears and not knowing *why*. She shut the door hard behind her and tried to forget it.

Now, when Henk returned, she began pressing him to fish the vase out of the pond. He was appalled at her state of mind. What was driving this woman, anyway? It took her weeks—frantic weeks—to convince him. But finally she wore him down, and he waded into the pond to find the offending article. After a long time he located it and headed back toward the apartment, wet and irritable.

Jan kept her distance from the thing as she instructed Henk to drop it into the cesspool. She remembered from Indonesia that hexed objects supposedly lost their power if they were flushed into raw sewage. Henk knew the vase was too big to go through the plumbing apparatus, but he was furious by now and he threw it in.

It disappeared.

Unamused, he gestured angrily toward its unseen destination.

"Let's not have any more of this nonsense, eh?" he spat.

Jan did not answer her husband. She was at rest. She could tell already, the vase's magical powers had been whisked away.

She was yet to discover that the spell had not been broken.

9

The Haunting

The army moved them into a real house on Kruizemunt Straat after several months. It was of typical Dutch construction, with a parlor in the front, a living room farther back, a kitchen in the rear, and bedrooms upstairs. In the narrow backyard was the *schuur*, a small brick storage shed. Most of their accumulated junk—and the trunk that came, finally, from Oom Theo—ended up out there in the schuur.

The house was back in the Arnhem area, where Henk had lived years before. His brother John, now known as Oom John because he was Johanna's uncle, came by occasionally to visit; he was working in the local brick factory, having buried his past by withdrawing from all talk of the war days.

Henk continued working long shifts away from home. The new house could have been a cheery place for Jan, the young mother. But it seemed gloomy to Jan from the start. As the sun set each evening, a chill fell over her, and a vague sense of fear settled in once again.

Nobody locked their doors in the Holland of the 1950s—burglary was practically unknown—and yet Jan feared that someone or some thing, was going to sneak into the house. It was not a phobia she could discuss with a neighbor; Europeans, she knew, didn't believe in the spirit world. But as each day drifted into night, Jan felt a heavy, evil presence lurking in the house.

As she sat in her bedroom upstairs, she found herself looking out the window into the backyard. There, the tiny window in the door of the schuur stared back at her like a solitary eye. Each time she glanced away, it drew her gaze back like a magnet.

Her heart pounded for hours, the anxiety boiling up inside her. There was no reason for this wild fear, she knew; and yet she knew the fear was very real.

What could be in that shed? Or in the house?

When Henk was home, it was different. He was a man without fear. If Jan ever broached the subject of evil spirits, he cut it off as nonsense. This was Holland, and to Henk it was a world away from the occult of Indonesia.

But during the long nights when Henk was away, that emotional bulwark was gone, and Jan found herself struggling to maintain some semblance of composure. Her eyes were pulled mysteriously, undeniably, to that little brick schuur.

Once again she caved in and compelled her husband to help her. She dragged him out to the schuur and asked him to look inside.

Inside was the big shipping trunk he had shipped to Oom Theo from Indonesia.

"Open it," Jan insisted.

Henk shook his head, annoyed, and threw open the case. Immediately Jan's eyes fastened on one of the objects inside:

a gem-studded dagger, the traditional Indonesian *kris*. Indonesians revered the kris as an object of black magic, but Henk like so many Europeans, had brought it from the islands as a valuable souvenir.

Jan felt the evil power pulsating from the object. She knew that in Indonesia the kris was said to have power and personality of its own. The older krises, it was said, could kill a man just by pointing at him. And the most powerful of the krises, according to Indonesian stories, sometimes flew from place to place under their own power, killing wildlife as they passed by.

"Please destroy it," she begged again, in a sad reprise of her earlier encounter with Henk's vase.

Henk argued but lost. He thrust the dagger under his belt— Jan winced—and he jumped on his bicycle. Several streets away was the Rhine River. There he hurled the dreaded kris into oblivion.

Still, fear dogged Jan mercilessly. The tiny window of the schuur still pulled her eyes into it from her bedroom window. Her stomach thrashed as she tried to hold the terror in.

But whatever it was—it was winning.

~~~

One night as she stared helplessly into the tiny square window, she caught a glimpse of a pair of eyes. She was terrified, but she could not look away. As she stared hopelessly, her eyes riveted to the window, she saw a small dark face come into view. It was smiling like a friend, but Jan felt cold. For long minutes they simply stared at each other, until finally the smiling face disappeared, and Jan buried her head in her hands and cried desperately.

"Jan."

She snapped to attention. It was an unfamiliar voice.

"Jan."

She whirled around, unable to tell where the voice was coming from.

"Jan."

A gasp escaped her. She jumped to her feet and looked around the room.

"Jan, come here."

Her head snapped back toward the window and she looked out at the shed. The smiling face was not there. But the voice was calling her to the shed.

"Jan, come here."

Her heart beating furiously, she pushed away from the window and dashed for Johanna's room.

"Come here, Jan."

Johanna lay sleeping calmly. Jan scooped the baby up with her blankets and hurried back toward her own bedroom. There she sat down on the bed, clutching the baby to her, rocking back and forth, squeezing her eyes shut and weeping in anguish.

"Stop...please stop," she cried over and over as the voice kept taunting her.

Until finally the tormenting spirit ceased to call her name.

When the quiet finally came, Jan lay down next to her tiny daughter and fell into tense, fitful sleep.

With her frazzled nerves, Jan was in no shape to maintain a delicate balance of relationship with Henk. They quarreled every day that Henk was home. He was tired of being angry with her, and that made him angrier.

~~~

The night shift approached again, and Jan felt the dread beginning to swell up inside of her. Henk left in the sunny afternoon; by dusk she was twitching with fear. The shadows lengthened, and her eyes began to search the gray corners of the house for something—anything—that might harm her.

It will kill you tonight! her mind screamed at her. *You must do something!*

She clutched her stomach and bolted for the kitchen. She threw open the drawers and gathered up the knives and forks—anything with a sharp point or edge—throwing them three and four at a time into her proper Dutch apron. Groaning incomprehensibly, she whisked to the parlor, still cradling the cutlery in her apron, and ransacked her sewing box. Every needle must be found, every pin disposed of. Get them. Hide them. All the yarn in the house—all the string, the twine, the rope—don't let him strangle you.

And finally she ran to the closet in the living room to dump her load. It was a standing closet cabinet, in the Dutch tradition, with a key lock. She slammed the door with the terrible articles inside, turned the key, and then hurried to the front door with the closet key still held tight. They had never locked the front door, but now she locked it and kept that key too. Clutching both keys, she ran to the dining room. By now she was panting. She locked the door to the dining room closet and kept the key. She locked the back door—another first—and kept the key.

Her heart pounding harder and harder, she flew up the steps. In each bedroom was another closet, another lock, another key to retrieve. When she had them all in hand, she took little Johanna and brought her to her own bedroom. She put all seven keys under her pillow and then lay down on it.

But the exercise brought no rest to her spirit. She lay awake, listening for the voice, straining to feel some alien presence drawing near.

The daylight hours, long a sanctuary for Jan's ragged nerves, now began to taunt her as well. Every sound on the street out front sent her scurrying to the door to see who was there. She jumped at the sound of every bicycle, every pedestrian passing on the sidewalk that ran along three feet from the front door. Nothing could hold her—she would drop sewing, feeding, anything—when she heard someone passing by. The urge could not be repelled.

It was never anyone she knew, never anyone coming to her place.

And as always, nightfall brought the old terror once again. After her next child, Henk Jr., was born, Jan took to sewing all night, sitting up in the children's room with all of them, away from the dreaded window, away from the shadowy schuur out back, away from the staircase that led downstairs. Her fingers flew, as if racing against the spirit world. But she could never win. Eventually the keys or the knives or the voices would drive her to frenzy.

It was time to do ironing. The children were asleep, and Jan set up her ironing board in the doorway of the tiny kitchen, with the laundry heaped nearby. She began pressing the iron into a shirt and glanced up. The front room light was burning but there was nobody in there. She set down the iron and stepped into the living room to turn off the lamp.

As the light went out, the breath caught in her throat. In the far corner of the front room, a figure was standing. The shadows enveloped him. His form was unclear. But Jan could make out the evil smile and the two piercing eyes. He stood motionless and silent. For long moments she was locked with fear. Finally, her mind flying wildly, she fumbled for the switch on the lamp and turned the light back on.

Instantly he vanished. But her stomach was tight. She knew he was not gone.

The front room became a place to avoid for Jan. As winter set in, the unheated front room fell into disuse. In the custom of Holland, everyone left their front room drapes open in the evening. With all the lights on, it was a pleasant diversion to walk down the street and see everyone's front room on display. But Jan drew her drapes, shutting out the rest of the world, curiously compelled to keep anyone from looking in. If she walked anywhere downstairs at night, she could sense the presence of that being in the front room, and her pulse quickened. Sometimes she did sewing or ironing on the ground level with Johanna playing nearby, and she began to notice Johanna staring toward the front room. But the child would never go near it.

And the horrible imprisonment dragged on. While Henk was gone, fear draped the house. While he was home, the tension—Jan's longing for a Christian home, and her confusion—still dogged them.

SCAN THE QR CODE OR

ENTER THE ADDRESS

IN YOUR WEB BROWSER

TO WATCH SAM RIJFKOGEL

EXPLAIN THE IMPORTANCE OF

RELATIONAL EVANGELISM.

WWW.TANGLEDDESTINIES.COM/VIDEOS/3

10

A Rebel's Farewell

"My friend Deetje van Sandvoort and her father want to take me to Amsterdam for an evening," Jan said to Henk one night. "Would you mind staying home with the children and letting me go?"

"No, that's fine," he responded. He was a kind man inside, embittered by the wars and embattled by his wife's strange quirks, but an unselfish person at heart.

Deetje's father, Mr. Regensburg, more than seventy years old, was a retired Pentecostal preacher. He was a Dutchman born and raised in Indonesia who had also fled to Holland in the Great Evacuation. He had taken Jan to his church a couple times in the past. It was a far cry from the starchy formal religions of most Europeans. In Regensburg's church were a small nucleus of free-worshipping outcasts from other groups— Dutch Reformed, Catholic, Salvation Army—who because of their Pentecostalism had no place else to meet. Now old Regensburg was gathering a busload to drive the three-and-a-half hours to Amsterdam to hear the famous American preacher Billy Graham in his first Dutch crusade.

Jan was looking forward to seeing the glitter of Amsterdam. She had never had an opportunity to play tourist and see Holland's sights. This would be great fun—and perhaps good therapy for her emotional stress.

The bus ride alone was therapeutic. Everybody sang songs and laughed and talked through the entire trip. Jan was in high spirits.

But then the evening went awry for her. The bus pulled into a huge parking lot and the group filed out into a colossal arena. There a great Christian rally swung into gear. There was singing and clapping of hands, and finally this Billy Graham stood up and began preaching.

Jan did not listen to him. She was calculating the odds. Would her group be swinging through downtown Amsterdam after this meeting—or was this it for tonight? She knew what was likelier to happen, and she was disappointed.

Suddenly Graham's words cut through her thoughts, and she heard him say, "The Lord is coming down for you. You can tell Him anything you want. Just come and tell Him everything."

Jan's mind froze on the word "Lord." In that instant she remembered that man, back in third grade, hanging on the cross in the Catholic school...that mysterious man who had made her feel so comfortable and secure. Suddenly she realized that He was the Lord—Jesus—this preacher was talking about...the Jesus that the Pentecostals had talked about. She had never made the connection before.

"The Lord is coming down for you."

Jan looked up. Before her she saw the glowing figure of Christ, radiant and shimmering. But as much as she wanted to gaze into His face, she felt Him pressing her forehead down so she could not look at Him. Three times she tried to raise her head, but each time the gentle touch of the Christ constrained her.

Without warning, she felt her face grow hot, and tears began streaming from her eyes, for no reason.

The preacher invited anyone longing for a relationship with Christ to move to the front of the place. Jan hurried, still weeping uncontrollably, hoping to get another glimpse of Jesus when she got there.

But no. All she saw when she looked up now was Billy Graham.

She was disappointed, but she was still experiencing a powerful transformation within.

"Bow your head," Graham was saying from the platform, "and just commit everything in your life to Him. Ask Him to forgive every wrongdoing."

Jan took the preacher literally. As she wept, her eyes shut tight, she went through a mental list. Her parents were first—she had disobeyed them so many times. Her tears intensified. Her husband was next—she had hurt him so much. She didn't want to cry, but she could not stop. Item by item, she turned her life over to Jesus Christ, encountering Him as a person, as the Son of the Living God, as her Lord and Saviour, for the first time. She could feel His touch inside her. She knew she had finally experienced what she was longing for.

Her friends from the bus had gathered around her to pray with her, but Jan was oblivious to them. She had forgotten all about Amsterdam. Hours later, as they all headed back home, she was still enthralled.

Henk was waiting up. He had fixed a little dinner for her. As she ate, she talked rapidly, full of zest, about her experience. Henk looked at her blankly. It was foreign talk to him. He could not grasp it. He asked questions. She tried to describe what she was feeling.

They talked for hours. In the deep of early morning, they were both finally exhausted. Henk stood up and stretched.

"You know, we usually fight when we talk," he said. "But we haven't fought tonight."

Jan grinned without a word.

The next day Henk left for duty, and Jan steeled herself for the battle once again. Tonight she would find out if the God who had touched her the evening before was really alive, really the one true God, her master and protector.

As dusk settled in, she did not collect knives and string, she did not lock doors and hide keys, she did not sit up sewing. She went upstairs and closed the bedroom door behind her and crawled in bed with Johanna and waited.

In the still night, sometime after midnight, she heard a door pop open. She recognized it as the door of the house. Someone—or some thing—was opening it, closing it, opening it, closing it, in an ominous, regular rhythm.

Jan lay in the dark of the bedroom, listening to the eerie metallic pulse. A voice whispered to her in the blackness.

"Why don't you go down and look?"

Jan held her breath momentarily before she heard a second voice.

"Why don't you just stay here?"

"No, go on down and see who is there."

Jan finally spoke. "I want to know if God is real."

Abruptly her right leg was lifted off the bed and her foot touched the floor. She knew she had to go. She stood up and opened the bedroom door.

Suddenly a bright light flooded the stairway, a divine light that filled the air but did not make her squint, and Jan felt the sweet, secure presence of her Lord.

She dashed down the steps and looked at the meter box. The door was shut, and nothing was moving. There was no one to be seen.

Jan turned around and walked slowly up the stairs. She was content. She knew her God was alive. She knew He was in control. Her fear disappeared.

―――

But there were problems and questions.

For a long time it bothered Jan that she had not been able to look at her Lord in the Billy Graham meeting. She timidly mentioned it to a couple people from the Pentecostal church—new converts, like herself, whom she felt comfortable with. But they knew no more than she did. Henk couldn't sympathize—he didn't understand any part of what had happened to her. She began reading the Bible, but much of it confused her, and it never occurred to her that Christ might not normally be visible. Her salvation was sure; she was confident that God had touched her. But she was still sad that she had never looked into her Saviour's face.

One afternoon she was kneeling in the living room, changing Alphons's diaper on the floor. Without warning, a light fell on the room. Jan looked up toward the picture window. There, hovering above her, was the Son of God. His face was completely obliterated by a dazzling brilliance. He sparkled like a million diamonds.

Jan could not contain her joy. She knew she was seeing the Lord Jesus Christ. She bowed her face to the floor and uttered "Hallelujah." It was a foreign expression to her; it was the first time she had ever said the word.

The radiant Christ moved toward her and reached down and touched her. She felt the love flowing into her as if it were electric current. She looked up again, longing to see His face. But she could still not get past the incredible light.

Then He vanished, and Jan was left to worship in quiet ecstasy. God had extended Himself to her again in His mercy.

Henk, trying to keep some semblance of equilibrium, agreed to go to church with Jan the first Sunday after the Billy Graham crusade. He was wary but willing—because obviously something had seized control of his wife and had powerfully changed her entire outlook on life.

They decided to go to the Dutch Reformed church Henk's mother had taken him to as a child. Jan thought the Pentecostal church the old man Regensburg had taken her to years before was a little too bombastic for her—and definitely too much so for Henk.

The dressed in their finest clothes and headed for the bus stop on foot. They were running a little late, and the bus put them off at the big imposing Dutch Reformed church after the service had already begun.

"Let's not go in," Henk suggested. "Everyone will just look around at us if we walk in late."

"All right," Jan replied. "We'll come again next Sunday and be on time." She looked at her husband, all decked out, and she smiled by reflex. Her emotional responses to him had been completely rewired since her conversion only days before.

"Let's go window-shopping downtown," she said playfully. Henk grinned boyishly and agreed.

It was while they were wandering through downtown Arnhem they found themselves in front of a building. Jan did not remember the place; she had forgotten its location—Regensburg had brought her several years before, and she was not familiar with the layout of the neighborhood. As Henk and Jan heard the happy singing inside, they decided together to explore the place.

Two Swedish missionaries, Sagstrom and Malmstrom, had begun the church. One of them was preaching when Henk and Jan slipped in at the back, unworried about being late because of the warm atmosphere the singing created. Jan ate up every word. She was hungry for more. After the service she went up to the preacher and asked him why he had stopped. Henk sat silent. He was moved, but he was determined to keep his composure.

As the weeks passed, the two of them attended the church together occasionally; sometimes Henk had duty and was unable to join her. Jan was enthusiastic; Henk was agreeable but aloof. He knew he was hearing truth, but he didn't want it for himself. He could still see his father's bloody clothes in the shipping box from Germany, and his mother's shredded scalp floating along the choppy Rhine. He could still recall shaking his fist in God's face and cursing Him unilaterally—and he still stood by those words.

But old man Regensburg had his eye on Henk. He wanted to see the serviceman accept Christ as his Lord. He asked Jan if he could invite Henk to a midweek service, and she approved. She would simply stay home that night. She knew Henk well enough to know that he would make a scene if Regensburg or the missionaries leaned too hard—and Jan did not care to subject herself to the embarrassment.

Henk sat passively through the singing and the preaching. He was moved but still unbending. After the service, Pastor Sagstrom approached him at the back of the church near the literature table.

"Brother, would you like to give your heart to the Lord?" he asked.

Henk's face colored up.

"No!" he shouted. He grabbed a Bible from the table of literature and hurled it all the way to the front of the sanctuary. "Because then I would be a liar!"

Regensburg later reported the incident to Jan. She was embarrassed. But she knew what it meant: Henk was too proud to take back his defiant curse of years ago.

The Pentecostals were unfazed by the incident. Within a few days they asked Jan if they could schedule a home Bible study in their home. She asked Henk. He shrugged his approval. These people were his friends—he just didn't believe as they did.

On a Tuesday night in the second week of September, 1954, all twenty-five church members turned out at Henk and Jan's little home. The living room was packed. Some were on the floor. The big easy chair had Henk and two others squeezed into it.

When the pastor asked everyone to kneel for prayer, Henk's eyes grew big with surprise. He had never seen this sort of thing. Even the fat pastor slid out of his chair and onto his knees.

For a moment, Henk sat alone in the big chair looking at everyone around him. He felt the pressure building within—the pressure to conform, but also the pressure to surrender to the Lordship of Jesus. Finally he decided it wouldn't hurt to kneel. At least he would be less conspicuous if anyone peeked during the prayer.

It was only a sliver of a moment, but in that fraction of time, Henk Rijfkogel was revolutionized. The moment his knee touched the floor, his heart instantly melted, and the Lord stepped gently in. In that incredible moment, Henk gave himself unequivocally to Christ. As his knee touched the floor, he could no longer resist the gentle beckoning of the Holy Spirit—and he belonged to Jesus.

And he did something Jan had never seen him do—he cried. Calling out aloud to God, Henk wept openly as the prayer meeting's participants joined him, praising God.

When everybody had left, Henk walked resolutely into the backyard, looked into the sky, and raised his open hands toward heaven, praising the Lord, thanking Him for His loving-kindness and His infinite mercy. God had never given up on him—from his childhood, when his dear mother's Christian witness prevailed; to his flight from Looveer, when the words of Scripture spoke to him from a wall plaque; to his months as a fugitive in the underground, when God kept him safe; through years of dangerous guerrilla warfare in the jungles of the Asian Pacific when the divine hand of God had covered him with safety; to this place, where he now was finally willing to accept that divine love.

Henk's decade of rebellion was over.

SCAN THE QR CODE OR

ENTER THE ADDRESS

IN YOUR WEB BROWSER

TO WATCH JAN RIJFKOGEL

DESCRIBE HER CONVERSION.

WWW.TANGLEDDESTINIES.COM/VIDEOS/4

11

"Hit the Baby"

New anguish came with Mirjam, the lovely fourth child of the Rijfkogel family. Into a home fresh with faith came this new daughter, her eyes oozing poison. Within a few weeks of her birth, doctors were sure she would soon be permanently blind.

Her eyes grew shut. Extensive medication produced no change. Doctors finally recommended desperation surgery— but it would have to wait until she was eight months old.

Henk and Jan, heartbroken, held fast to their fledgling faith. They believed that God could heal their tiny, helpless Mirjam. It was a new sensation, this faith, but ironically it was the most realistic hope for this presumably hopeless situation.

Surgery was scheduled, but Jan set about to have her miracle. She made a practice of praying in her own bedroom, then running to Mirjam's bedroom to see if the impossible had occurred. But the terrible oozing always continued. Back and forth between the two rooms she stalked, praying her simple prayer almost by rote, wondering how all of this was supposed to work, and holding out less and less hope. Jan had not yet learned to distinguish faith from curiosity.

Finally Tante Stoter, a loud woman from the Pentecostal church, chastised her.

"My child," she declared condescendingly, "if you have any faith, the Lord will heal her!"

The words, self-righteous though they were, pierced Jan's heart. She returned to Mirjam's bedside alone and prayed a different prayer.

"Lord, she is your child. If you want to heal her, please heal her. I am leaving her in your care."

And she walked away from her baby.

The torment disappeared, and Jan stopped the desperate routine of prayer and prognosis.

Henk always left the house early in the morning to teach a class at the military base. His practice was to check in silently on each of the four children before leaving.

This morning, for the first time, he saw no ugly fluids caked around Mirjam's swollen eyes. Perhaps...but he would wait and see, rather than get his wife needlessly anxious.

Mrs. Ruster, a Catholic Indonesian woman who lived across the street with her cynical husband and a huge, fat Chihuahua, stopped by later in the day to visit with Jan. As she peeked in at the baby, Mrs. Ruster was surprised to see Mirjam's face clean and bright, her eyes apparently normal.

"She didn't have her surgery already!" Mrs. Ruster half-asked, half-stated.

"No, it's not for several months," Jan replied, a smile creeping across her face as she realized the miracle that had taken place—and so quietly, so simply.

Mrs. Ruster was flabbergasted by Jan's version of the case. God? Healed this child? She reported the bizarre story to her husband.

"Just wait until surgery day," he shrugged, cocky and confident. "They'll be wheeling her in for that operation, you'll see."

But the cure was complete. Mirjam's eyes opened normally, and she began to take in the sights. Word spread through the neighborhood that the Rijfkogels were saying God had healed their baby of blindness.

Mr. Ruster held out for the rational odds. But surgery day came and went. He and his wife, overwhelmed by what they had seen, gave themselves wholly to Christ, accepting Him as their personal Lord and Saviour.

Henk and Jan, still baby Christians themselves, were gleeful.

———

The evil spirit would make one final stand against Jan.

A fifth baby, Emmanuel, had come along. According to Dutch custom, children went to bed at 7:00 p.m. and were left home alone with Johanna as babysitter when the parents went to church on Sunday. In the winter, Jan put Emmanuel in the typical Dutch cloth sack and tied it up around his chest to keep him from kicking it off. Then, to warm him, she used a *kruik*, the traditional round metal container, filled with boiling water. She would normally wrap the hot kruik in a heavy cloth and situate it next to the baby's feet.

But this Sunday evening, as she began to wrap the kruik, she felt a dark impulse inside herself.

"Hit it," a voice seemed to say.

Jan was jarred. She loved her children. This was so alien to her.

"Hit the baby."

She held the kruik in her hand and looked down at the helpless infant. She was terrified and confused. It was a heavy container when it was full like this. She knew she could kill the baby with a single blow to the head.

"Hit it," the inner voice stressed again.

Jan swallowed hard and placed the kruik next to the baby's feet. Her insides were convulsing.

"I can't go to church," Jan said flatly as she walked into the bedroom.

"What's the matter with you?" Henk asked. "You're shaking."

"I don't know; I don't want to go to church."

She did not yet perceive church as a place for help and healing; she felt she had to be in complete working order before she got there.

"You're already dressed and ready to go," Henk insisted. "Now all of a sudden you change your mind. What happened?"

She dared not tell him.

"What are you struggling for?" he demanded.

Finally he persuaded her to go.

They were late.

The church, now located in a former Coca-Cola building, was L-shaped. At the main entrance was a little alcove with only a few chairs. It was out of the view of the rest of the sanctuary. The pulpit, at the intersection of the two rooms, was visible to people in both areas.

Henk and Jan sat in the smaller area, just inside the main door. The pastor was already preaching. They had barely settled into their chairs in the alcove when the pastor stopped abruptly in the middle of his sermon.

"Devil!" he shouted. "Get out of that person, in Jesus' name!"

Jan looked up sharply. She felt her shoulders jerk forward, and as she watched, a gaseous black ball lurched out of her chest and floated away from her. It was more than a foot across, vague around the edges, but dense and ominous. Time was momentarily suspended for Jan as she watched the thing circle halfway around her and then disappear through the door.

Jan began praising and worshipping the Lord—and the church service became a simple old-fashioned prayer meeting. Henk sat by, stunned. He had not seen the black ball, but it was clear that something phenomenal was happening to his wife.

That night she explained everything to him—the old fears, the encounters with the evil spirit, the knives and needles, and this final experience. Henk wept with her as she recited the years of agony. When she was done, he held her close.

For them, the holocaust was over.

But they had brought a new generation into the world.

~~~

Christianity did not solve every problem or smooth every rough edge. The two new believers found their everyday faith was challenged in very practical ways. Bickering often broke into their lives. Jan still had to struggle with her temper. When she grew angry with Henk, she often blew up into a rage.

"Is this what it's all about?" Henk asked suddenly one Saturday as Jan expressed her anger. "This churchgoing, this Christianity? Is this it? Do you give your life to Christ, and still have the same problems?"

Her face darkened, and she began railing at him furiously.

Henk gestured toward her. "Come on up, devil," he called out, with a hard edge in his voice. "Come on up and fight with me."

Jan grew angrier. He was making an ugly suggestion—as if the devil were inside her.

As they sat in church the next morning, Jan's ears perked up as the preacher told a story.

"I heard yesterday," he began, "that the devil was coming against somebody, bringing out the old nature in that person, and someone challenged the devil to come out of that person and fight him.

"Now, friends," the preacher continued, "that's a mistake. You never challenge the devil to fight you. Instead, you should plead the blood of Jesus over that person."

Henk had tuned in too, and by now he was red-faced with anger. It was obvious that Jan had tattled to the pastor. The service was barely concluded when he marched to the pastor and demanded to know who had told him about challenging the devil. The pastor replied that a friend had told him the incident—nobody Henk knew.

"It was me," Henk shot back angrily. "You were talking about Jan and me. I told the devil to come up out of her and fight me fair and square."

The pastor was compassionate. Jan had not talked to him at all, he explained. God was just teaching the two of them day by day how to live and grow in Him.

But in spite of their new faith in Christ, Henk and Jan found they lacked much power when it came to dealing with their tough old human nature. One Sunday morning a flyer was distributed at their church admonishing the people not to be late for service. Jan bristled. With five small children to collect and prepare, she was often late. She jabbed Henk and snorted at the flyer as it came to them in the service.

She was still irritable hours after service ended. At 4:00 p.m. she and Henk were having tea at a tiny table in their backyard, seated on either side of a teapot, two cups, and a tray of cookies—and she brought up the subject angrily.

"Oh, that thing wasn't written for us," Henk responded calmly.

"It was too."

"No, it was for people who are late all the time even though they don't have little children."

"Nonsense. We're always the last ones to arrive." She was seething. She saw her husband siding with the pastor instead of her.

"I don't think you need to worry about it," Henk consoled her.

Jan pounded her fist on the table. It toppled over, strewing the pot and cups and cookies all over the lawn.

"I'm not going back to that church again!" she shrieked, standing over him. "You can go if you want, but you'll never see me in that church!"

Henk began picking up the clutter.

"Well, I'm sure not going without you," he said in a matter-of-fact way. "I don't want to have to answer all the questions about where you are and why you're not there. I'll just stay home too then."

"I don't care. I've made my decision."

They sat home that evening. Jan stewed. Life went on, but there was a dull tension in the house. Jan was hurt and angry and worried by turns. She did not mind crusading herself, but she did not like the idea of being responsible for Henk slipping away from the Lord. Still, she had made such a big deal about never going back—what could she do about it now?

On Tuesday morning, one of the ladies from the church knocked on the door while Henk was out running errands.

"Where were you last night?" she asked Jan. "We had a great meeting with the American preacher."

"I forgot," Jan replied. In her anger, she had completely forgotten about the American evangelist who was to hold nightly meetings in their church during the entire week.

"I'll pick you up for tonight's meeting," the woman said cheerily.

"No…I'm not going."

"Why not?" the woman asked in surprise.

"I'm just not." Jan looked at the floor.

116

"Yes, yes, you are," the woman answered with a smile. "We'll be here. You be ready."

Jan did not tell Henk. Her Chinese pride did not allow for her to lose face and take back her angry vow. Henk would be leaving for night duty that afternoon. She could sneak out to the service and he would never know.

The meeting was not held in the church. They were meeting in a garage on the outskirts of town, trying to establish a new work in that neighborhood. Ironically, Jan and her friend arrived late. Jan stopped at the back of the room.

"Come down front with us," her friend suggested. There were seats available in the front row.

Jan declined. She felt filthy. She felt unworthy of the front row. She stood quietly in the back while everyone else praised the Lord noisily.

Throughout the service she poured her heart out to God, confessing her shame at having accused the pastor, and attacking her husband, and challenging their commitment to the church.

The American preacher was inviting people to pray for baptism in the Holy Spirit, for increased spiritual power in their lives. Jan had no intention of moving to the front, but as the altar call was made, she felt her spirit moving steadily toward the front. She opened her eyes in surprise—but she was still sitting in her seat. She closed her eyes again, and as she did she began bubbling forth in an unknown language, praising God and being filled with the Holy Spirit. The entire congregation was swept up in the presence of the Lord, and they all worshipped together for a long time.

Afterwards Jan stood up and—for the first time—testified in public of her faith in Jesus Christ. Her Chinese reserve was stripped away, and she told the people the story of her anger over the flyer, her attack on Henk, and how God had dealt with her mercifully.

Now she faced the test. She went home and waited for Henk to return. He always came back from night duty in a state of fatigue because of the long hours, but nevertheless she greeted him with exuberance. She told him joyfully about what had happened, and Henk rejoiced with her. He had not wanted to quit attending church. He felt too great a difference between his old life and his new life—it was a difference he did not want to give up. And, in spite of his exhaustion, he wanted to attend the next evening's service with her.

The tidal wave swept over Henk that night. He was gloriously filled with the Holy Spirit, praising the Lord in an unknown tongue.

But still, life somehow did not become paradise.

12

Miracles

In the Dutch tradition of obsessive cleanliness, Jan was accomplishing part of her spring cleaning by beating the dust out of her carpet runners with a broom as they hung on a tall steel pole. It was a beautiful morning, the sun only barely up and the typical overnight fog fast burning away.

A Royal Dutch Army captain walked up to the house with a flat, grim expression. He was unaccustomed to this sort of duty, and clearly uncomfortable in it.

"I have to give you a message," he offered tentatively.

Jan exhaled sharply. "Is it bad?"

"Your husband has been in a wreck."

The next hours were a whirlwind, as Jan rushed off to the hospital, leaving cantankerous old Tante Stoter from the Pentecostal church to stay with the children. The children heard the news that their father had been a passenger in a jeep that had struck a tree in the middle of the dense rural fog the night before, but they had trouble comprehending the consequences. They knew only that they had been left behind with crabby Tante Stoter—who forced them to eat everything on their plates, and whose wide rear end was often the target of their imaginary darts.

By the time Jan got to him, Henk's leg had already been encased in plaster and suspended above him. His pride, more than his body, was damaged. It would be weeks before he could be up again, pursuing his usual dynamic schedule.

Henk grew more and more restless as the weeks dragged on, as he passed the one-month mark. A numbness began to seep through his injured leg, but the doctor insisted he was imagining it. When finally, after six weeks, the cast came off, Henk's foot was completely paralyzed.

The cast had pinched a nerve.

The smug doctor suggested therapy in a distant rehabilitation center. Henk would have to admit himself for two weeks at a time, only spending every other weekend at home. And the travel was tiresome in itself, on top of the pitiful limp that now marked his walk.

Summer faded; autumn faded; winter set in. As the holiday season approached, Henk grew weary and discouraged. He wanted to be healthy—and home—for Christmas with his family.

"Well, Lord," he finally prayed one day, exhausted by the ordeal, "I am your temple. If you want to live in this crippled temple, that's up to you. But if you don't, then heal me. I'd like to be home for Christmas."

Within a few days of Christmas, the numbness in Henk's foot suddenly disappeared, and his gait returned instantly to normal.

It was a Christmas for a special rejoicing.

Johanna, the firstborn, was fond of riding her scooter with her friend Anne Marie to the *winkels,* the string of little stores that served as the hub of commerce in postwar Arnhem. First stop for Johanna and Anne Marie was always the meat market, where they teased the butcher for pieces of liverwurst. Depending on the lard content from day to day, sometimes the girls enjoyed the stuff, sometimes they didn't.

In front of the butcher shop was a sewage grating, through which the girls could see a rich variety of lost *dubbeltjes* and other small coins, lying just out of reach. Johanna had perfected a technique of tying soggy, sticky chewing gum to a string and dropping it through the grating to capture the dubbeltjes. Then the girls could go to the fish market and buy their treats—raw herring, the beloved snack of the Netherlands, which they held by the tail and gobbled all the way down. And, if the booty from the sewer was big enough, they could get some salted licorice as well at the nearby candy store.

But every neighborhood has bad kids, too, and Arnhem was no different. One of the bigger boys often loitered in front of the winkels to harass the young girls. One beautiful bright summer day, he was waiting for them as they scootered down the sidewalk. They saw him in their path, and Johanna hoped he would leave them alone.

He looked like he might, until the last moment, when he stuck his leg in front of the scooter and threw the girls sprawling. Anne Marie tripped and recovered. Johanna fell, her leg twisted under the scooter, unable to get up.

The winkel owners and customers came running. Someone took off for the Rijfkogel home, where Henk was taking an afternoon nap before night duty. Soon Henk was scooping Johanna up in his arms, comforting her and praying for her and heading for the doctor.

It was a complicated injury, one that the medical men could only speculate about. Johanna's leg was placed in a cast, and she made trip after trip to the hospital for treatment and tests. The grim doctors scared her; Henk always had a cheerful word of encouragement for her.

But finally, the doctors insisted on surgery.

Henk and Jan began to pray in earnest that God would heal their daughter. Surgery was scheduled, but the family agreed in faith—as they had with Mirjam years earlier—that the operation would not be necessary. As the surgery date approached, Johanna's condition did not improve.

The day before the operation, Henk picked Johanna up out of her bed and carried her to their church. Pastors Malmstrom and Sagstrom and several of the church people placed their hands on the little girl and prayed for God to intervene in a miraculous way.

The next day Johanna was wheeled into the hospital. The doctor examined the leg and looked up at Henk and Jan, puzzled.

"This leg is completely well," he said softly. "There is no need to operate."

Once again, the Rijfkogel family had been touched by the divine hand of God.

As they grew in faith, Henk and Jan were happier and more content than they had ever been. Their family continued to grow, with Johanna and Henk Jr. and Alphons followed by Mirjam and Emmanuel and Samuel. Their father was fond of taking the older children on hikes on Sunday afternoons. Sometimes they explored the dikes or the old brick factory where Oom John worked or the old farm homes or the restored World War Two battleships in the river. Sometimes they brought home a chicken or a rabbit or some other delicacy for Mother to cook up. Sometimes they bicycled the mile or two to Oom John's house in Huissen. Henk's brother had married a Dutch woman and they had three children of their own by now. The places that had held such grim memories for Henk were now a source of delight as he showed his wide-eyed children where his ferry had docked, and where the great battles had been fought, and where the bombed church steeples had still not been replaced even ten years after war's end. And they rode their bicycles over the long Rhine bridge—the bridge Henk's mother had died for—to the beautiful park at Sonsbeek.

They even vacationed—something Henk had never taken time for in his entire life. One of Henk's old Indonesian friends had located his wife just outside Haarlem, in the western part of Holland, and the Rijfkogels decided to spend a few days with them.

It was a lovely house, standing at the edge of a beautiful park, but still conveniently close to the main highway. It was also, they discovered—to the sheer delight of the Rijfkogel children—a house full of bedbugs. The woman of the house was a great source of ridicule for Johanna and her brothers and sisters—a short, dumpy woman with slick black Indonesian hair pulled into a bun on the top of her head.

Haarlem was something of a tourist attraction, so Henk and Jan decided to take the three oldest children out for a whirlwind tour one evening. Johanna, Henk Jr., and Alphons got ready to go and went outside to play in the park while they waited for the adults.

Suddenly, Alphons, the youngest, dashed toward the highway. Johanna's eyes followed him—and then spotted a huge truck carrying a load of cement barreling toward him. Before she could even let out a scream, she watched the truck swerve wildly and knock Alphons into the air like a soccer ball.

A lady pedaling by on a bicycle had seen something spinning away from the truck and thought it had lost a tire. She pulled up to the body just as Henk Jr. and Johanna ran up, shrieking hysterically. One of Alphons's shoes had been thrown yards away.

Henk and Jan came running across the park from the house, with Jan grim and silent, and Henk compulsively muttering to himself in a state of near trauma: "If God takes Al…if God takes away one more thing that I love so much…if God takes Al…"

In his mind, the houseboat was being annihilated all over again, and his father's bloody clothes were being taken from their Red Cross box.

The parents approached and stopped short of the body. It was clear the boy was dead. He was not breathing and not moving.

Henk looked at Alphons evenly, unable to collect any rational thoughts, barely able to call out the name of his Lord for help.

Even then, it was a whisper: "Jesus," Henk rasped.

Instantly Alphons cried out, and continued crying loudly. The group standing and kneeling around him were stunned, but in a split second they began shouting joyously. Soon a doctor had arrived and moved Alphons into the house, where he could not find any evidence that an accident had occurred.

"This boy just needs some rest," the doctor declared, looking around at the jubilant houseful. "But he sure won't get it here! Let him come to the hospital for observation."

By the time the children were allowed to visit their brother in the hospital, only a short time later, Alphons was running around his bed laughing and playing and wanting to get out of the place.

For Henk, it was a milestone. He had seen firsthand how fundamentally life had changed since he had made Jesus Christ his Lord. His eyes were opened to the power of Jesus' name. From that day on, Henk communed with his heavenly Father day by day, minute by minute. Worrying ceased for him. He knew, finally, he could place his life—and the lives of those he loved—in the Father's hands.

It was a long way from the houseboat.

13

Visitor

Johanna grew to love Sundays as the day of great activity in the week. In the summers they rode their bicycles past the winkels, over the Rhine, to church; in the winters they walked to the bus station and took a bus to church, while Johanna gagged on the ever-present cigar smoke. But it was still adventure for her.

The children played around the flower garden in the front yard, and along the path to the schuur out back, bordered by tulips and white and purple lilacs.

On Sunday night Henk and Jan put the children to bed at 7:00 p.m., still according to Dutch custom, and went to church alone. Johanna as the oldest child was deemed babysitter—which amounted less to sitting than sleeping.

Lying in her bed, Johanna could feel a subtle shift in the air one evening as her parents left. The house fell silent, except for the soft breathing of her brothers and sisters, and in the darkness she could feel a new presence, a dark presence. She had fairy-tale pictures displayed on all the walls of her room. Tonight it seemed they danced to life.

Then a man stepped into her doorway. He was dark and large, silhouetted in the twilight. Johanna could only stand to look at him for a few seconds before she rolled over against the wall and began screaming. There was an open window next to her bed that looked out directly on the next house only inches away. She knew Tante Annie next door would come running to help her if she screamed loud enough.

But something snuffed out the sound. The neighbors did not come. The other children did not stir. Only Johanna could hear her own frantic screaming.

And when she finally had the courage to peek back toward her bedroom door, the figure was gone.

She was scared to tell her parents. She swallowed the fear instead.

The terror returned the next Sunday night. The dark shape of a man appeared in the doorway again. Johanna clutched her blankets and pushed away from him, until she was pressed against the window. She screamed again and again, but no one could hear her. And finally, again, the figure drifted away, leaving the child gasping and crying.

"If you are a child of God," the Swedish pastor said every Sunday morning, "you can plead the blood and tell the devil that you are a child of God." It was a favorite theme of his. Johanna heard it the next Sunday morning and determined to use it that night if she had to.

As she and her father pedaled home from church together on their bicycles, Johanna silently rehearsed the words—"I'm a child of the King. I plead the blood of Jesus." With the wind whipping past her as her bicycle flew down the Arnhem streets, Johanna felt the tension rising. Pumping the pedals up and over the great Rhine Bridge, she could feel the confrontation coming.

That evening Henk and Jan tucked everyone in and slipped out of the house on schedule. Johanna waited breathlessly in her bed.

Endless minutes passed. Nighttime settled over the house.

Johanna turned on her side, her back to the door, and waited.

Softly, the figure appeared again in the doorway of her room. She could feel him looking at her. Slowly she turned over. Her heart skipped, and a lump grew suddenly in her throat. She could see a nose and a pair of eyes, but no features. There was no scowl, no smile—just an intent stare that chilled her all the way through.

In the back of her throat, a terrified scream begged to escape. But she kept swallowing it furiously, desperate to stay in control. Her mind was swirling, grasping for the words she had rehearsed.

The burly figure stood motionless in the doorway, waiting, as if he could wait forever.

Johanna finally pulled the words together in her mind and threw herself out of her bed.

"Devil, you get away from me," she spat, pointing at him defiantly. "I plead the blood of Jesus over me. I'm a child of the King!"

Breathing hard, she stood her ground and watched for his response.

The figure stared a moment longer, as if mildly surprised or puzzled, then turned slowly and walked out of view.

Johanna dumped herself back into bed. She was jubilant but exhausted. She could feel the air clearing. The devil was gone. She was a child of the King, fully protected—she could sense it.

She slept soundly, and burst out of bed the next morning to spill the entire story to her mother.

"A man was coming in my room—a devil."

Jan looked at her sharply.

"He would always scare me."

Jan felt her stomach tighten. She had not seen or heard anything of the spirit world for several years.

"But last night I told him what pastor said," Johanna babbled happily. "I told him I was a child of the King, and I pleaded the blood of Jesus, and I told that devil to get away from me."

Jan's eyes brimmed with tears.

"And he went away, Mom!"

Jan took her little daughter in her arms and held her close. She knew in her heart that the war had finally been won. Satan had tried to continue his onslaught against yet another generation of her family, but he had finally come up against a greater power—in the hands of this fragile little girl.

"That devil will never bother you again, Johanna," Jan assured her quietly, holding her tight. "Jesus will protect you. You did well."

SCAN THE QR CODE OR

ENTER THE ADDRESS

IN YOUR WEB BROWSER

TO WATCH JOHANNA GARRISON

EXPLAIN HOW TO OBTAIN

VICTORY OVER EVIL SPIRITS.

WWW.TANGLEDDESTINIES.COM/VIDEOS/5

PART III:

AMERICAN DREAM

14

Amerika

Henk enjoyed the Sunday afternoon street meetings. At about two p.m. people from the church would gather on the main street in downtown Arnhem and sing songs and testify to passers-by about the goodness of the Lord. Many of those who passed by on Sunday were the young servicemen Henk was training to kill during the week. For some of them, it was strange to see their superior officer in civilian clothes talking about the love of God after such a gruesome week's work. But it was even stranger for Henk.

Month by month, the military life fulfilled him less. He hated his work—training young men in the art of killing—and he hated the foul-mouthed atmosphere of the base. Time and time again he came home and told Jan about his encounters with young men under his authority—servicemen who had asked him about his weekend ministry—and the discrepancy between what he was preaching on street corners and what he was teaching in camp.

But he could not get out. He had signed on with the Royal Dutch Army for life. The only way out was to find a job that paid at least as much as the government paid him—an impossibility in Holland in the late 1950s.

Or, they could leave the country. Henk and Jan looked at their children, growing up so quickly. More than anything they wanted their children to have opportunities to learn and to minister in the Kingdom—and yet those opportunities seemed limited in Europe. There was not even a Sunday school in their little church. The great Sunday schools, the great Christian schools, the great churches—the big spiritual advantages—all seemed to be in *Amerika.*

And finally, deep down inside, Henk did not mind the idea of leaving Europe. It was not really home for Jan either—she had never seen her parents since leaving Indonesia—but for Henk, Europe held no fascination.

They began to think and pray about moving. It seemed on one hand a far-fetched idea—and yet on the other it was only another location; they had both made such an adjustment before, under unhappier circumstances.

Once again, governments took destinies into their own hands. President John Kennedy signed a new immigration law into effect in 1961 which allowed Indonesian people who had evacuated to Holland to move to the United States. Henk put their names in for consideration when he learned of the law. But it was too late. The allotted places had already been filled.

They thought about Australia. It was close to Indonesia, but European in quality. But the door was open only to European couples. Jan's Chinese blood disqualified them.

And Indonesia was still not a wise choice. There was still, after more than ten years, the old animosity for the Dutch.

Three hundred years of colonial rule could not be forgotten in a mere decade.

Then, abruptly, the Kennedy government re-enacted the law, and the names on the old waiting lists were contacted.

The letter said that if they would fill out the enclosed paperwork the New York-based Church Work Services organization would arrange for a church somewhere in the United States to sponsor them. Henk filled out the forms and sent them in. And they waited.

It was a strange limbo. Henk was in night school to get another promotion. The children were in school and life went on. But every day there was the breathless sort of waiting... waiting for word to come. Were they accepted? Would they be moving to America?

Johanna and the older children were aware that a move was in the works—but it was always talked about tentatively. The younger children were not told.

Suddenly all the speculation was over. Henk came home with a letter in hand. They had been accepted for sponsorship by a Presbyterian church in Garden City, Kansas. They had to be on the steamship *Maasdam* in Rotterdam at 4:00 p.m. in exactly two weeks, on February 26, 1961.

Alphons was scheduled to have his tonsils out in a few days. He would be getting out of the hospital only a couple days before departure. They decided to go ahead with the surgery. After all, what if the arrangements fell through and they ended up not going? Alphons would still be stuck with his bad tonsils.

By reason of the same uncertainty Henk did not resign his post with the Royal Dutch Army. He stayed in his night-school course as well, working steadily for his promotion as if nothing had changed.

But Jan was busily distributing furniture and other belongings to friends and deciding what to sell and what to take over on the crossing. The Dutch government was picking up all costs, but there were space and weight limitations. Jan looked long and hard at their big upright piano. Some of the kids were just beginning to play it—and Henk and Jan were thrilled. She decided they would lug it over with them.

The children were excited. All of them but Alphons, who was in the hospital, watched the house steadily empty of its holdings. What novel entertainment!

When Alphons came home, he was stunned. He had not been told about the move; it was decided the hospital stay might go badly for him if he had moving on his mind. As he wandered through the nearly vacant house, his hand went compulsively to his head, and he began pulling at his hair. For hours he tugged at it, silent and wide-eyed, until handfuls of hair began tearing out at the roots. Jan tried cajoling, comforting, punishing. Nothing could stop him. The moment he was out of her sight, he began venting his confused insecurities by pulling out his hair.

The day before the ship was scheduled to depart, Henk completed his course and received his promotion. Now a major in the Royal Dutch Army, he promptly resigned. He was happy. Finally he could be a full-time Christian.

The next day the family bid Oom John and their cousins and friends a final farewell. Oom John was sad to see his brother go, but he concealed it. He knew Henk to be the aggressive brother, and he could sense the enthusiasm Henk had for the new adventure.

As they walked up the gangway to the *Maasdam,* Henk and Jan could not help but remember their similar walk in Jakarta ten years before. It was so different now, though—with the children, and with Christ walking alongside them.

They would learn months later that they had been included in the exodus by an accident of governmental bureaucracy, that Henk did not actually qualify under the law because he had never been an official resident of Indonesia. But by now, Henk and Jan's destinies were out of their own hands and in the hands of Another.

The trip was a delight for everyone except little Alphons. He was still in shock, still pulling his hair. After eleven days they docked in New York harbor, in the classic shadow of the immigrant's heroine, the Statue of Liberty. As everyone prepared excitedly to leave the ship, a United States health officer made his rounds.

"What is wrong with the child?" he demanded of Jan in a stern voice.

Everyone turned to look at Alphons. In a glaring three-inch area, he was completely bald.

They stayed on the ship an extra day, until a doctor could certify that Alphons was not suffering from a disease.

He was only suffering.

They were installed in Garden City, Kansas, in the care of Pete and Lois Drevnick at the First United Presbyterian Church. They expected to find cowboys and Indians in the Great American West, but they were pleasantly surprised.

None of the Rijfkogels spoke any English, but they plunged in, determined to learn and to do for themselves everything they possibly could. Henk was determined not to give Holland a bad name in the United States.

They had no car, no house. Their sponsors, Lois and Pete, helped them find an apartment and a job for Henk at the local co-op that paid $1.15 an hour. Lois faithfully took Jan shopping and taught her virtually everything about American life. There were gaps, of course. When Jan planned to have company for the first time, she chose a frozen pie, something she had never seen before, and served it straight from the freezer. The entire group, including Henk and the children and, eventually, Jan, exploded with laughter.

Sometimes they ended up playing a ludicrous game of Chinese telephone. One day Jan sent Johanna to the market to buy *stacks*. The butcher was confused. What were stacks? He sent Johanna back home to get a description.

She reported back to him in a few minutes.

"Stacks. You know," she explained, "good meat."

The butcher laughed heartily and packaged some steaks for her.

Johanna was enrolled in the local grade school in April, where the teacher put her by herself and handed her a blue textbook—in English, of course. Johanna dug in, determined to learn this crazy new language. She learned fast. A girlfriend named Cynthia walked her home each day and helped her expand her vocabulary and improve her spelling by pointing at objects and asking Johanna to name them and spell them.

There was the inevitable teasing: Johanna's shoes looked funny to Kansas children, and her accent was thick at first. But by and large, Henk and Jan could see the grace of God enveloping each of their children as they adjusted to this new land.

There was never a day of doubt or discontent. No struggle with the language or the customs could make Henk or Jan look back longingly toward Europe. They were completely locked in by their confidence that God had led them to this place. When the church ladies said something she didn't understand, Jan smiled and nodded. She was content—and humbled by their kindness to a twice-displaced foreigner.

Jan was slow to learn English. She could not seem to grasp an understanding of what she heard. She was not discouraged, but she desperately wanted to learn. In her direct, childlike way, she knelt down one day by herself and asked her Lord for comprehension of English.

The transformation was remarkable. She began to pick up meanings and sentences immediately.

But she still had trouble speaking the strange new language. Above all she wanted to communicate, so she could tell her sponsor, Lois, about her Pentecostal experience—something that Jan was surprised to find lacking in the Presbyterian church. Again she knelt privately in prayer. Again God honored her faith-filled request. Soon she was speaking English clearly. One day she sat with Lois and recounted her entire baptism in the Holy Spirit—a thrilling achievement of communication for Jan.

Soon the Rijfkogels moved across town to the Pentecostal Assemblies of God church, where they could feel freer in their worship. They walked to church or had friends pick them up. Henk bicycled to work. Soon, however, the people took up a collection to buy the Rijfkogels a car. It was an old blue-and-white Chevy, just in time for the harsh Kansas winter. Henk did not want to accept the charity, but the men of the church prevailed. And Henk was truly thrilled; he had never owned a car.

At the Assemblies of God church the ladies had a weekly prayer meeting. Jan began attending immediately and enthusiastically. Then one day she realized they took turns leading devotions. She looked down at her Dutch Bible, the only Bible she ever used. As they read in English, she followed the meaning in Dutch. But someday soon, she knew, they would call on her, and what would she do then?

A third time she prayed for specific, practical help. Her eyes were illuminated. She was soon reading English. When her time came, she stood before the group and read a text of Scripture and gave her testimony—all in precise English.

Every day, life was fascinating. Henk secured a better job with the farm co-op, running seed-processing machinery. It was smelly dirty work, something he had not done since his antiguerrilla days. For years he had been a sharp, proper Dutch officer. Now he came home each evening with his green mill uniform and his hair and face covered with grain dust, reeking of corn and sweat. But he was willing. He felt God had something better for him, but until that day came, he was willing to work at this.

The kids started music lessons again, and Henk and Jan were still able to store away a little bit in savings. They acquired a black-and-white television set, so their kids wouldn't have to climb all over each other for a peek through a neighbor's window, as they had in Holland.

For five years, the Rijfkogel clan plugged away, absorbing themselves into the American way of life, right down to speaking English over dinner. The children grew strong, physically and spiritually.

But the American dream was not yet quite complete—and not yet shattered.

15

The Final Journey

Even with six children, even with low pay, even with music lessons all around, the Rijfkogel savings account had fattened just enough to buy out a local janitorial service in the spring of 1966. The owner wanted to move to St. Louis. Henk saw the chance to be his own boss—and perhaps even employ some of his own family. The American Dream.

They began with twenty buildings. They cleaned floors and carpets in the daytime and did the rest of the work in the evenings. The community's confidence in the business grew steadily, and the work increased.

They had been living in an ancient house on C Street, and with each ritzy house he cleaned, Henk prayed that God would help him provide better housing for his family. No one was complaining, but Henk was anxious to give them all the convenience of modern American life. Within the year, the Rijfkogels had moved up the hill, from C Street to B Street, into a beautiful new home.

It was the great American success story. They all studied and became naturalized United States citizens. Jan began leading a girls' group called Missionettes in the church. Each child made Henk and Jan proud. Henk Jr. joined the U.S. Army. Johanna was voted Miss Garden City in 1972 and later went away to a Christian university in Missouri. Henk's notoriety as a businessman and his enthusiastic witness for Christ carried him into the speaker's rostrum at Rotary and Lions Clubs and other meetings all over western Kansas. Everywhere he appeared, Henk faithfully and forthrightly declared what Jesus had done for him—throughout his life—and for his family.

But the American success story was about to be abruptly rewritten.

On a November evening in 1972, Henk left with Emmanuel and Alphons in the van, just as he did each weeknight after supper. They would head first to nearby Pierceville, Kansas, to clean the Channel 13 building, then back to Garden City to do the YMCA. They usually returned home by eleven p.m.— if not, Jan worried.

This night she began glancing at the clock at ten p.m., wondering where they were. It made no sense, but she had a fluttering in her stomach.

She had held a Missionettes meeting in the basement of their home the night before, and she was sorting their crafts and materials when the phone rang. It was just before eleven.

It was a hospital staffer, calling to report that her son had been involved in an accident.

"Which son?" Jan asked quickly.

"Emmanuel."

She knew Henk never left the boys by themselves on their rounds.

"Where is his father?" she asked.

"I don't know," the voice responded. "We only have the boy here."

"Tell me what has happened."

"I'm sorry, ma'am. You'll have to come down here to the hospital and sign some paperwork first."

Jan hung up and began racing. She told Mirjam, who was sixteen, that Emmanuel had been in some kind of accident and she should stay home with the younger children till she called from the hospital. Esther, the baby, and Samuel were both sleeping.

Jan dashed to the hospital and screeched to a stop out front. There were a dozen steps leading up to the door, and she ran up without a break. She leaned into the door; it was locked. She would have to pull around to the emergency entrance on the side of the building.

As she turned to go back down the steps, an invisible shroud fell over her, silently, heavily. It hung on her as she slowly descended the stairs.

―――

The sweet-tempered Mennonite farm people of the surrounding areas lived off their cattle. Too often they failed to keep them fenced. The sheriff had warned Farmer Koehn to keep his cows off the Pierceville Road. A Corvette had gone into a ditch trying to avoid one of his cows a couple weeks earlier.

The Pierceville Road, like all the other stringy roads connecting Kansas' tiny towns, was unlit. Alphons was driving. Emmanuel sat next to him, and Henk was on the passenger side.

By the time the headlights picked up the form of the cow in the road, it was too late to slow down. Alphons whipped the steering wheel to the right to avoid the collision.

The van jumped like a stunt car and bore into the earth. The concussion exploded the windshield. The metal was wrapped around Henk's legs and held him fast. Emmanuel, crushed by the vehicle's hulking engine, was splattered over his father and unable to move. Alphons was crunched under the steering wheel, but he pulled himself out through the open front of the wreckage. The gnarled, twisted van had completely buried Henk and Emmanuel. Alphons circled the mess wildly, screaming for his father. By the time a car pulled up at the scene, Alphons was in a complete frenzy, babbling incomprehensibly.

Two hospitals were called. There were none nearby. The Dodge City ambulance arrived, and the fire department personnel cut a hole in the wreckage to pull Henk out. He talked to his sons through the entire process.

"Alphons, you take care of Emmanuel. God will heal me…no Emmanuel, you're strong, you're all right."

Alphons, shattered, rode with his father to the Dodge City Hospital. The Garden City ambulance arrived and took Emmanuel. In the emergency ward, the attending doctor determined easily that both his legs were broken in several places, along with dozens of other cracks and splinters. They would require surgery the next day.

"Call his mother," the doctor said, "to sign a release."

~~~

Jan dragged her feet as she entered the commotion of the emergency area. The heaviness she felt was like a drug. Every movement was a chore. She leaned against the wall until one of the ambulance drivers noticed her.

"Who is in there?" she asked.

"Emmanuel," the man answered. "I just brought him in."

"What happened?"

"There was an accident on the Pierceville Road, out in the country. There was a bend in the road and they were going to hit a cow."

Jan looked at him evenly. "Where is his dad?"

"There is no dad."

"Surely there was a dad in there."

"It was dark, ma'am, and there was so much commotion."

"There must have been a dad," she insisted.

"I heard the other boy calling 'Pa! Pa!' I thought it was his grandfather."

"That's my husband. Where is he?"

"Must have been a Dodge City ambulance, ma'am."

That would be miles away, Jan thought.

"Someone inside the van was saying, 'Emmanuel, you're strong, you're all right.'"

Her eyes brightened.

"He sounded real strong, ma'am," the driver offered.

Dazed, Jan called her pastor. He hurried to join her.

"Where is Henk?" he asked as soon as he arrived.

"They said they took him to Dodge City with Alphons," she replied wearily.

"Then we'll call Dodge City."

The pastor placed the call. The hospital personnel said they had no information. He hung up, frustrated. In a few minutes he called again, demanding to know about Henk Rijfkogel.

"He just passed away."

⁓⁓⁓

The Dodge City hospital was crowded, and Henk's stretcher was delayed on the hospital steps. Alphons paced and trembled as his father drifted away. Henk kept telling Alphons not to worry about him—"Take care of Emmanuel; God will heal me"—but finally unconsciousness overtook him.

Henk stopped breathing before he got inside the hospital.

Alphons had no recollection of the Garden City ambulance taking Emmanuel. For all he knew, his mother was still at home with Mirjam and the other kids, worrying about him.

Numbed by panic, Alphons called his house. Mirjam answered. She had not yet heard anything from anybody.

"Dad just died on the hospital steps," he told her.

⁓⁓⁓

Jan's mind swirled aimlessly as the pastor told her Henk had died. She had completely forgotten about Mirjam and the other children at home. She tried to call Henk Jr. at the military base in Georgia, but she couldn't get through. The pastor began trying to reach Johanna on campus in Missouri.

The moment Jan walked into the house was the moment she remembered Mirjam. She began to tell her, but Mirjam cut her off.

"Alphons called me already, Ma," Mirjam said blankly. "He told me."

━━━

Johanna thought it was strange that her pastor would call at two in the morning. There were no phones in the rooms. She took the call in the dorm director's apartment.

"Your brother Emmanuel was hurt in an accident with the van tonight," he began gingerly.

Johanna knew the nightly routine all too well. "What happened to my Dad?" she asked immediately.

The pastor sighed. "He was killed."

When Johanna hung up, she stepped into the laundry room around the corner from the phone. It was too much to comprehend. He was so full of life, such a joy to his friends and acquaintances—and his family.

She stood there for a long time and grew furious. It should have happened to anyone else, but not him. He had conquered so much to be beaten this way.

━━━

He was forty-six years old. Newspapers carried his story. He had spoken all over western Kansas, giving his testimony and sharing the love of Jesus Christ, and now the stunned populace paid him homage.

The funeral could have been a time of anguish, but as the Christians gathered they found themselves rejoicing for Henk's sake. Johanna, Mirjam, the rest, all knew he was in heaven.

Still, each child grieved privately, each for a different length of time, each in a different way, before coming completely to terms with the loss. Esther, a first grader, could barely grasp the fact that Daddy was gone. She was hurt, and did badly in school for a while.

The youngest boy, Samuel, was confused, but he rebounded just as he knew his father would have.

The older children rarely spoke of their personal feelings.

Mirjam was silent.

Henk Jr. never mentioned the loss.

For a long time Johanna fixed her anger on the Mennonite farmer, but eventually the healing balm of forgiveness soothed her. She determined to tell her father's story and declare the goodness of the Lord to her generation—just as her father had begun to do.

Emmanuel never learned about his father's death until after Henk was buried. A medical prisoner, his entire body encased in heavy plaster for six weeks, he could not have stood the strain. He walks with a limp to this day.

Alphons withdrew completely. He had driven the doomed vehicle. He was tormented by it. He was fragmented, lost, convinced of his own worthlessness. For months after the funeral, he could be seen standing alone at dusk, pulling at his hair. His anguish nearly consumed him, until through the patient support and personal ministry of Johanna and other members of his family, he began to gravitate back.

Jan was strong. Her God had some greater purpose, she was sure. She would rather have grown old with her Dutch serviceman, but she would survive and live for the Lord nonetheless.

She found strength, as she had so often, in praising and thanking her Lord.

PART IV:

FULL CIRCLE

16

Where We Went

Henk was supposed to come home that fateful November night. The children's father should have come home to them, tired from a night's work, and Jan should have welcomed her husband and tried to make sure he had enough to eat and sufficient rest.

But that would be in a perfect world, and they did not live there yet. Instead, the children's father did not return, and the provider who had taken care of his family did not come home to his wife. The Rijfkogel family was at a crossroads after Henk's death, and their choices were not easy ones.

How would they survive? How would they pay the bills?

Alphons had heard Henk's final words, which were a prayer—not for himself, but for his family: "God, take care of my wife and children." Henk was a man of faith, and he did not doubt that the God in whom he so strongly believed would indeed answer this prayer.

But how?

Jan came home on a cold November day with a son in a full body cast still in the hospital, another blaming himself for the wreck, and her husband in heaven. Everyone was hurting. To whom could she turn?

Jan clearly heard in her spirit: "Praise Me and thank Me, even in this situation." It was her strongest help and confidence and strength, and those words from God stuck with her. She began to praise and thank God nonstop. She did not know how they would make enough money, but she knew that God was good. He would provide.

Every day and every night, Jan clutched her Bible close and praised God. And there she gained her strength and the victory—which she has kept to this day. "In every situation," she told her children, "we can still give praise."

One night, Jan awoke from her sleep and didn't know where she was. Alone in her bed without Henk's steadying presence beside her, she did remember one thing: to praise and thank God! This conviction was so strong, it persisted within her waking and sleeping.

"God will cover us," she said repeatedly.

―――

Young Alphons faced an uphill battle, blaming himself for the accident. As the one driving that cold November night, he felt burdened with guilt. He was with Henk when he died but escaped serious injury himself, and it was hard on this young nineteen-year-old.

Sometimes he would go into the backyard and pull out his hair in anguish. He saw his brothers and sisters at home with no father, and he felt responsible for their loss.

God is truly close to widows and orphans, and Jan trusted Him with her family. From Alphons blaming himself to Emmanuel's recovery from his horrible injuries to Johanna's battle with bitterness, Jan faced family issues without Henk as her support.

Difficulties did not wait for the family to mourn. While dealing with the difficulty of burying Henk, she was confronted by a disturbing feeling that someone Johanna had been dating wasn't right for her. One night, Jan woke up and saw a vision of him, and then she understood that he wasn't really who he was claiming to be.

A woman from church encouraged Jan to plead the blood of Jesus over him anytime he came around. Instead of directly confronting him, she prayed. Though Henk wasn't there to shepherd his daughter, Jan knew that her daughter's heavenly Father was there, looking out for her.

In a short time, the man Johanna was dating stopped coming around, the relationship was over, and Jan's prayers were answered. Even with no husband, her children still had a Father.

―――

Of all of the family members, Johanna, especially, wrestled with anger against the farmer, who had been warned repeatedly to keep his cows on his property but who had failed to do so that night. His negligence had indirectly caused her father's death. It was a difficult time—and a true test of the power of God to heal and bring forgiveness.

A battle raged in her heart between bitterness and forgiveness. She saw the sheriff reports of previous warnings, and asked questions of the most reputable lawyer in town. Could her family sue the farmer for his negligence? Though his family had money, they hadn't offered to help hers. Could this be a way of *taking* the help the family needed?

Because of that area's small rural population, the lawyer felt that Jan wouldn't stand a chance of obtaining financial help from a jury of the farmer's peers. Johanna painfully realized that no help was going to come from these people who had money, but who showed no interest in helping a widow and her seven children.

Johanna faced a choice not that dissimilar from her father's so many years before in World War Two when he watched the tragic death of his family and the hatred of the Nazis. Henk wondered why God hadn't protected his family. "Why should I have faith in a God who does not protect His people?" he kept asking. For years that question made him bitter, and it took many years for God to soften his heart.

After coming to salvation, Henk developed a theology of life and suffering—life is hard, but God is good. Life is unjust, but God is always just, and He is sovereign. Now, Johanna faced her own questions about evil and suffering in the world, with her father unfairly taken from her and her family. What conclusions would she reach?

She had to deal with the anger and the influence of friends who were lawyers, filling her thoughts with what the world thought *should be*. Forgiveness was not their focus. But Jan knew that it must happen, and she prayed.

Johanna later shared what she had learned with her mother: "Trusting is not an emotional thing. It's an *act*. Are you going to do the right thing and trust God? It's a bigger thing than just *saying* that you trust God—will you *behave* like you do?"

It took time, but the Lord did a healing work in Johanna's heart.

On Jan's part, she didn't hold a grudge against the farmer or even think he was at fault. She simply thanked and praised, for again their heavenly Father had counseled His children and walked them through a difficult time.

―――

Jan had no family to turn to in the United States, no financial help was forthcoming, and Henk's thirty-thousand-dollar life insurance policy would not last long in a family with seven children. But what she did have was a strong work ethic—and Henk's janitorial business. What had started as Henk and some of the older children's business now fully became a family business—everyone would lend a hand, even six-year-old little Esther!

Jan was a strong, resourceful woman. She would make it, she decided, and would not resort to living on the insurance money when she could work. Jan owed nothing on their house, which comforted her, and she did not want to put her faith in the life insurance money. Hard work and faith would see the Rijfkogel family through, not a check that would run out over time. Putting the money aside in an account, the family pulled together and all went to work. As a result, Jan didn't spend a penny of the life insurance! Ever!

It was sometimes hard not to look at what other people had and desire it, but God always answered Jan, "Have I not provided?" And that was enough for her.

As a widow with no husband, making ten dollars an hour, Jan watched as God provided for her family.

SCAN THE QR CODE OR

ENTER THE ADDRESS

IN YOUR WEB BROWSER

TO WATCH JAN RIJFKOGEL

SHARE HOW GOD PROVIDED FOR HER

AND HER SEVEN CHILDREN AFTER

HER HUSBAND'S TRAGIC DEATH.

WWW.TANGLEDDESTINIES.COM/VIDEOS/6

With no family in the States, the Rijfkogels spent a great deal of time at church, both before and after Henk's passing. One Sunday less than a month after Henk passed, Mirjam sang a beautiful song that served to encapsulate how the family felt about their Father in heaven.

The pastor asked Mirjam to sing a special song, and that song was "Through It All" by Andrae Crouch. It was so fitting for this trying time—in every situation, God had indeed brought them through. The song filled them with confidence that they would come through stronger for having learned to trust in Jesus even more than before!

Emmanuel, who was still recovering from his injuries, remembered that song and it changed his life going forward. Only fourteen when his father passed, throughout his life he spent far more years trusting the Lord as his Father than trusting his earthly father, Henk.

Johanna, who played for her sister that Sunday, felt the strength that already pervaded the family. They all seemed to understand that they were never victims because of circumstances. Life can be unjust, and things are unfair. Trouble will come, they knew. But the question for them became: What would they do with it? How people of faith respond to difficult circumstances is a thread throughout the Bible, but this practical question became like a motto for the whole family.

"It's like God asked, 'What will you do with the circumstances you encounter?'" Johanna recounts of those days. "God allowed it, and those who believe have a choice: trust God and His Word, or doubt His goodness and plan for your life."

Even in this dark time, the Rijfkogel family understood this at some level—though they still may have been coming to terms with it as Mirjam sang about God's presence with them *through it all.*

However, for Jan it never seemed to be much of a "choice" at all. She simply trusted God.

~~~

Some years later, Alphons encouraged Jan to move into a new house. She saw a new house nearby, but she didn't know how she could get into it and out of the old family home.

"Lord, that would be nice," Jan prayed. With no husband, she trusted God to provide for her. With Esther and Samuel still at home, and others coming home frequently to visit, she wanted a newer home with more room. Yet, she refused to force this change.

God helped Jan buy that new home in 1980! Finding it too small over time for all the growing family members as her children made her a grandmother, she later added on to the house to make more room. Jan did not want to leave debt to her children, but God gave her peace to get a loan for the addition, which increased her payments at the time. A friend suggested she combine the loans, and when she refinanced, the new home and addition's payment was the same as her first mortgage!

But Jan didn't want her children to have to pay off the home and addition for her, so she asked God for help to pay off the loan. With the small amount she was able to make per hour and the very little Henk's Social Security provided, Jan worked very hard to leave an inheritance to her children—not a debt— by paying down the principal each month.

A wealthy eighty-year-old woman for whom Jan had worked passed away. Jan had served this woman dedicatedly for years without a complaint and always with a good attitude. When the woman died, the accountant administering her estate sent Jan a letter.

But Jan, thinking it was junk mail, set it aside, unopened. A week later, he sent her another letter, but she didn't open that one either. Finally, he sent a third.

Esther was already married but came home from out of state to visit Jan, and she happened to see the envelope. She told her mother to open it. She experienced the joy of watching her mom open the letter—together they learned the great news that the wealthy woman had left some money to Jan in her will because of her years of loyal service! No one else outside of the family received a dime, but Jan got the perfect amount—just enough to pay off the loan for the home and its addition!

~~~

In some families, the history of faith left by the parents falls apart in the children. But this was not the case in the Rijfkogel family. Jan's greatest desire was that her children would serve the Lord in spirit and in truth. She did not seek position or recognition, but she persevered in prayer that all of her children would serve God.

Johanna graduated from Evangel University and came home to help with the family. She was the first to go to college, which was important to a recently immigrated Rijfkogel family just trying to survive. But while no one said that she needed to come home to help because things were going poorly, she felt her family needed her. She ended up getting a job as a teacher in her hometown, which let her be there for Esther, who was up late with the family janitorial business even when she was very young. It had been two years since Henk had died.

Johanna met Alton Garrison when he came to speak in their home church in Kansas. Alton, a single evangelist in his late twenties, knew it was customarily not accepted to date during a revival meeting. However, when he met Johanna he decided to ignore that custom. Because of his travel schedule, their opportunity to be together was sporadic. If the relationship ever seemed to wane, Johanna's sister, Mirjam, was always there to play counselor. Mirjam's prayer was playfully, "God, let them fall in love!"

Alton and Johanna married after a year and a half and as of this writing they have celebrated thirty-seven years of marriage and ministry together. After several years as evangelists, they served as pastors of First Assembly of God, North Little Rock, Arkansas; served as Arkansas District Superintendent; and have been the Executive Director of U.S. Missions. Presently, they serve as Assistant General Superintendent of the Assemblies of God.

Henk Jr. was in the Army when his father died, and he never forgot the day he received a call from Pastor Bryant informing him about it. The Red Cross flew him home from Vietnam. The flight home was one of the most peaceful he had ever been on. As the oldest son, with all his other brothers in school, he was later released from military service in order to take up the family business. He was twenty years old at the time, and he helped run the family business for decades to come.

A church leader and a Royal Rangers leader since 1965, Henk Jr. served as a mentor to future Christian men, helping build the foundation of faith for other generations.

"I can speak for all my brothers and sisters," Henk Jr. says of his life of faith, "when I say that we would never do anything to discredit my mom and dad. They were the people with the greatest faith I have ever seen in my lifetime." He cites how his father handled difficult people, conflict in the church, and hard work as setting an example for him to follow, which he does to this day. "God will handle it," he remembers his father saying over and over.

Alphons, known as Al to the family, also worked with Henk Jr. and Emmanuel in the family business for many years. Business partners and friends as well as brothers, they all worked hard to support their families.

Al became a musician, playing the violin. He did not receive professional counseling or church help after the car wreck that took his father's life, but could often be found playing his violin which seemed to comfort him in his grief. It amazed his family to watch the way God preserved him and restored him. Although the family didn't talk about the wreck and Al's difficulty with it, his sister Johanna was sensitive to what he was going through and helped him process the tragedy.

"God knew all this would happen," she told him. "Do not beat yourself up over this." And slowly, Al dealt with his loss.

"Do you ever think about the crash?" Johanna asked him years later. "Not really," he answered. He seemed at peace and was able to talk about it in a matter-of-fact manner. Though this came many decades later, it let her know that Al was okay.

Quietly faithful Mirjam met her husband, Steve Laird, while he was in Bible college. After getting married, the two began living out a terrific testimony. They planted a church in California. Planting a church always has its financial challenges.

God had sustained Mirjam in the past and miraculously came through again. He provided a way for them to build a beautiful home on a piece of land someone gave them. Today Mirjam serves as a children's pastor and has always enjoyed praising God in worship, which demonstrates a stark contrast between her shy demeanor and her confidence while singing onstage.

"She has so much faith," Jan says of Mirjam, "no matter what her circumstances are." When Mirjam encountered struggles in life, Jan noticed how faithful she was and sometimes asked how she handled them. "God provides," Mirjam always answered.

When the truck crashed that fateful November night, Emmanuel had been sitting on the van's third seat, which was really just a motor cover. Emmanuel's injuries from the crash were very severe. He went through a long, grueling rehabilitation period, and one leg was shortened in repairing the damage from the accident. Emmanuel had a limp after the wreck—and does to this day.

However, despite his injuries, Emmanuel's youthful spirit was not dampened. When the pastor came to cheer him up, it was instead fourteen-year-old Emmanuel who cheered up the pastor!

Emmanuel served as a junior high Sunday-school teacher and on a church board for many years, bringing a hardworking Christian witness to the children in his class. A farmer for a long time, he first faithfully served the family business as soon as he was able to help. His wife, Cindy, is a noteworthy sportswoman in barrel racing, rodeos, and other competitive sports.

The youngest brother, Samuel, entered the ministry early, serving as an evangelist for twenty years. Sam preached in hundreds of churches in the United States and overseas. A divine move of God in First Assembly of God, Grand Rapids, Michigan, resulted in him staying there for four years as their evangelist. In 2005, four years after their revival, he and his wife, Brenda, became the pastors there. Thousands of people worship every week in that thriving congregation.

Fun little Esther, the baby of the family, was the only Rijfkogel born in the United States. With fifteen years between her and Johanna, the oldest, Esther was a bright and cheerful ray of sun to a family dealing with life's most difficult issues. When Johanna returned from college, the two became closer, with Johanna as almost a second mother. Partners in many adventures, including Johanna's dates, Esther was a source of cheer for the whole family.

She later married Dave Williams, a businessman from Nebraska and successful, prizewinning professional rodeo roper. The couple's quarter horses are also noted award winners. Esther and Dave have twin miracle boys, and their conception and birth tested Esther and Dave's faith. For a time during the delivery, it looked as though they might lose them both before Esther brought those two precious little boys into the world and the danger passed.

Then, a couple of days after the twins were born, the doctors told Esther and Dave that one boy may have Down syndrome. Their faith was not shaken, and they continued to pray for their miracle babies, together with the whole family. Today, both sons are accomplished and award-winning rodeo ropers like their father, and neither shows any evidence of the difficult circumstances of their birth.

Jan worked steadily and with dedication, simply showing her family her testimony through hard work and deeply ingrained faith and values. She has worked into her eighties, for years cleaning the church by herself.

Jan has never faltered in trusting God all the long years since Henk's death. Whenever anyone comments on her faith or her family, she beams with gratefulness when noting that her children have not departed from the inheritance of faith left by their parents.

Family get-togethers are large and noisy, with the seven children, spouses, and twenty-five grandchildren and great-grandchildren. It's quite amazing that an immigrant family with no relatives in the United States has developed into such a tribe. Everyone gets along surprisingly well and all enjoy one another's company. Now spread out across five different states, the family does not get together as often as Jan might like. But when they do, gatherings center on *food*. In typical fashion, Jan takes great pride in laying out a peerless spread of food and Asian-inspired hospitality. No matter how many hours she worked beforehand or her advancing age, Jan cannot be dissuaded from cooking the most delicious Indonesian food and making each get-together a feast.

"If I'm going to have my children come," Jan says with a twinkle, "I spread the whole table! I cook late into the night, and the next day I clean."

Though they all may not live close enough to meet frequently, it doesn't stop the family from lifting one another up in prayer whenever a need arises. Their new generations of grandchildren and great-grandchildren don't always fully understand the extent of what Henk and Jan went through individually or what the family experienced together. The grandchildren have had their troubles, and divorce has rocked some marriages. But the bond between them all remains strong.

On a less serious note, grandchildren and great-grandchildren can come to family gatherings without any experience with Indonesian food!

"They either love it—or they're out!" Henk Jr. jokes.

The family has a tendency to be practical rather than overly sympathetic or coddling, and Johanna sums up the reason for it nicely: "We have great empathy. You've got to have a moment when you cry. But then, what are you going to do?"

Jan can always offer an answer—the same one she has for decades.

Give thanks, and praise God, no matter what!

SCAN THE QR CODE OR

ENTER THE ADDRESS

IN YOUR WEB BROWSER

TO WATCH SAM RIJFKOGEL

EXPLAIN THE POWER OF WORSHIP

DURING TIMES OF LOSS.

WWW.TANGLEDDESTINIES.COM/VIDEOS/7

17

Full Circle

Jan didn't know what the future would hold, but she knew whose hands it was in. "After Henk's death, I did not know what my children's future would be. But I did know one thing: it was my responsibility to lead them to be who God wanted them to be. That was my main thing. I prayed, 'God, use them as you see fit—not what I want for them—and let them all serve you in spirit and in truth.'"

She was amazed how God answered those prayers. "I cannot believe that God would love me so much and do so much for me! My children all love the Lord and are serving Him!"

"We came from nothing; we had nothing. And God made everything right for us," she says as she looks back at God's faithfulness. "I just cannot thank Him enough. I am amazed by His love, grace, and mercy to me."

Today Jan's greatest blessing is that her children love and serve the Lord and that some have gone into the ministry, even though she is just a humble woman who cleans for a living. "I was pushing a vacuum when I learned that Samuel would be pastoring a church. Lord, how could you be so good?"

"Who will lead them? Who will guide them?" she remembers asking God.

God answered the same way He had for decades: "I will lead them and direct them. *I Am* their Father."

And that was enough for Jan.

———

At no point did the Rijfkogel family accept the feeling that they were victims or the mentality of a victim. They asserted that a person's circumstances can never make one into a victim. Yes, life can be unjust and unfair. Jesus Himself told His followers that in this life, trouble would come.

And again, the question is, "What will you do with it?"

The Rijfkogels chose hard work—they chose to put their heads down and get to work, to not feel sorry for themselves, and to press on. Difficult years came and went, but the family members each decided what they would do when those trying times came: work hard and trust God. Even when working late into the night compromised the younger children's schoolwork, everyone contributed and everyone worked very hard. Even when marriages rocked or grandchildren wandered, they trusted God.

And they made it.

Through her hard work and faith, Jan taught the children that they needed to collaborate with God. They understood the temptation many face to take on a victim mentality, where they feel out of control and as though bad things are happening to them that they cannot change. But the Rijfkogels learned that hard work and a victim mentality are mutually exclusive.

Jan had little, but she didn't accept a negative mind-set or an entitlement mentality, where she thought someone owed her something. She simply worked hard—and the kids did too, right beside her.

If you are able bodied, you work—this was the strong belief in the Rijfkogel home. No handouts, no self-pity, no excuses. Just good old-fashioned hard work. Jan's choices impacted the whole family and drove home a strong ethic that has served each one of them their entire lives.

At the time, Jan didn't think about the inheritance and work ethic she was instilling in her children; she simply did what she had to do. To her, sitting back in defeat and accepting a handout was never an option. She wasn't putting on a show; her hard work was a natural response to the situation she was in.

"It's so real to her, the things she did," Johanna recounts of those days. "She had such a consciousness of God's position" as Provider, Counselor, and Father to her children—even as Comforter.

"My mom's faith," Henk Jr. adds, "was just as fresh after my dad's death as it was when she first came to Christ in Holland and as it is today. It has not changed. It's as though her faith has been renewed; it just keeps going."

Henk Jr. continues, "When she talks about how important praise and faith are to her, we're tempted to tell her, 'Yes, Mom, we've heard this before.' But it's true. That faith that my mom and dad had is the legacy that they have left us, their children. It's the same legacy I want to instill in my children."

Legacy, the Rijfkogels showed through their actions, isn't *what* is left behind. It's *who* is left behind—the people who live in the spiritual inheritance left by those who have gone before.

Jan and Henk's faith is still fresh today, as is their legacy.

Alton Garrison, Johanna's husband, notes that people have a tendency to say, "If God were really good, why would He let that happen to me?" and, "Well, you don't know what I've gone through" as excuses for acting a certain way.

"But when hearing the story of Jan and Henk, and understanding what they went through after Henk's death, it becomes hard to say those things. You can't experience much worse," Alton says of the struggles his wife and her family went through. "You can't complain in their presence!"

"I never heard either of my parents complain," Henk Jr. recounts of those early years in America, of his father's death, and of the many years since. Instead, "My parents were servants—they were always willing to help, from the church to the community," Henk says.

Like many hardworking families, the Rijfkogels have demonstrated over the years that they do not believe in entitlement. It certainly was not within the family mind-set to blame the farmer whose cow caused the accident that took Henk's life. For years since, they have accepted the farmer's neighbors and relatives as clients in their cleaning business. Henk Jr. notes, "And they know who we are, because there aren't too many Rijfkogels around!"

This testimony of hard work and excellence has opened doors for forgiveness and for the family business that bitterness and self-pity would certainly have squelched!

—*###*—

Jan knew that her spirit before being saved was completely different than the Spirit she received when she was saved. She was truly born again—out from a spirit of fear and into a spirit of peace! Jan came from a Buddhist background, though something in her heart fell in love with the Man hanging on the cross that she had seen early in her life. Little did she know that looking up at that Man and loving Him would open a door of grace into her life; nor did she understand the impact that it would have as it reached out beyond her own life to that of her husband's, her family's, and beyond.

With each of her children serving the Lord, Jan looks back at that open door of grace and thanks God for the generational impact of her walk with God. She remembers battling the inheritance of fear she received from her biological family so that she could take up the inheritance of peace she received from her adoptive Father, and today the fruit of having fought and won that battle continues to grow and develop.

"My transformation," Jan says, "from a non-Christian and from the demonic influence I came from, and my husband's transformation from a person who did not believe in God at all because of the situation he went through in World War Two, shows that God changed us 180 degrees. But we had to trust Him."

Jan knows that she faced a choice. She could either do what God asked her to do, or she could go the other way. She chose to accept God's goodness however it came to her, and to accept His presence and blessing, even when times were hard.

———

So many seemingly coincidental events happened within this family, starting with Jan and Henk meeting each other, then being apart for so long, and then meeting again and marrying. Their destinies were intertwined over the course of years, but this was only a beginning, and Jan never wavered from believing that divine appointments were orchestrating their lives.

Even Jan's attendance and salvation at the Billy Graham one-day crusade in Amsterdam was a scheduling miracle. Billy Graham had stopped holding one-day rallies overseas because of the expense. But the people of the Netherlands were so persistent in asking him to come, he broke protocol to go to Amsterdam for one night—the very night that Jan saw a vision of Jesus in the crusade and was saved.

"Just think," Billy Graham said much later, smiling widely. "We weren't even supposed to be there." Then he winked and went on, "But you don't believe that, do you?"

Repeatedly, God showed His hand of providence in leading Henk and Jan to where they needed to be, when they needed to be there—even before Henk repented and came to Christ!

———

Many years after Henk Rijfkogel watched his family die in the tragic Allied bombing on the Rhine, his daughter, Johanna, along with Alton, Jan, and Alphons and his two children all returned to Holland and even visited the church Henk and Jan had attended. The current pastor was just a boy when Henk and Jan were raising their family there, and he and Alphons remembered playing with toy cars together. It had been fifty years since Henk and Jan had moved their family to America.

Alton had been invited to speak at a conference in Holland and was able to speak in the church that Jan and Henk had attended so long ago. Now in a different location than when the Rijfkogels attended, some fifteen people still remembered Jan and her family and welcomed her back.

While there, they were able to reconnect with Marie, Henk's brother John's wife. They were able to talk and catch up on how much had changed in fifty years.

A visit to a war museum deeply moved them all—especially a display on Operation Market Garden, the horrific tragedy that cost Henk and so many others their families. The son of the Swedish pastor who had led the small church there in Holland when the Rijfkogels lived there gave them a tour, which helped bring closure to some painful memories.

The Rijfkogels had come full circle to where Henk had lost his family. Though he had come to terms with his faith in the face of that great loss and was now gone from this earth, finally learning some of the details that contributed to the disaster on the Rhine brought healing to Jan and the others.

In the aftermath of the bombing, Henk had shaken his fist at the sky and vowed that he would never bow his knee to the God who had let his family die. Many years later, salvation followed when Henk finally broke that vow and dropped to his knees. For years he had struggled against the gentle beckoning of the Holy Spirit and had keenly felt the lack of peace in his soul. But with that one act of surrender, he let forgiveness deliver and release him from the prison that he had constructed.

His powerful story of release and forgiveness really hit home to his family while visiting Holland. Henk's heirs were able to see how his bowed knee had so profoundly affected their future. He had been forgiven, yes, but he had also forgiven the people who bombed his family, and freedom reigned for the rest of his life.

Henk knew he would never get justice for his family. After years of fighting, he decided to let the Lord deal with it, and peace was the outcome.

When faced with the question "What will I do with it?" regarding his unfair circumstance in life, Henk's answer for years was bitterness, unforgiveness, and a lack of peace. But when Henk let go, everything changed! The children saw the evidence of change in his life, for Henk became a person who forgave.

He was a man set free, truly revolutionized, and the man of faith he became left a heritage of faith and freedom to his family.

"He drifted around without God so long," Jan says. "But I think because of the prayers of his mother before she died, God followed him. He was under conviction, but he refused it. When he went to war, he saw so many people killed. And when he met me, he thought all Christians were hypocrites." But Jan so wanted to meet the unknown God she had seen as a girl, the one her husband wanted nothing to do with, that she says she "trusted through it all, because I wanted to serve this unknown God."

God honored that desire and the prayers Henk's mother had offered for him before she died. Both Jan and Henk would indeed find the Lord, forgiveness, strength, and the faith to persevere through hard times as God wove their tangled destinies together into His plan for their hope and future.

~~~

Henk left his family with ways to remember his love for them. Johanna held a booklet of notes, like a poetry book or journal, especially closely. Henk had written in it when Johanna was only seven years old, and he had written letters to Johanna and Henk Jr. for two years before he was killed. Henk didn't know that he wouldn't be there to read it with them, but he wrote poetically of the Lord—words that have kept speaking in his voice long since his family laid him to rest. He wrote it in his native Dutch, and its strong theology and rich description of the love of God has helped his children understand their father's depth of faith and love—for his Lord, and for them.

"He talked of the love of God," Johanna recounts of this journal. "It wasn't something ethereal to him. He wanted us to understand how much he loved us, but he was even more passionate about how much more our heavenly Father loved us."

Yes, Henk also wrote of obedience to God's Word. But he wasn't dogmatic, trying to get his children to act right so they would get rewarded. He shared how rewarding it was to live God's way—to do good, be kind, show mercy, and act justly.

Coming from Henk, once a hardened soldier who survived both the Nazis and the jungle warfare of Indonesia, these poetic words of love and goodness left his children with a testimony far outliving his time with them.

In the Dutch language he wrote, "The path of life is not always easy or a bed of roses; but always trust that God will be at your side." In another place he wrote, "Just look back, and you will always see that God was walking with you."

Storms will come. Trials certainly came to the Rijfkogel family, and while Henk didn't know how long his words would outlive him, he nevertheless left a testimony to his children that has comforted them long after a trying storm took him away. God gave Henk a new outlook on life—one with the understanding that troubles will come but he could be positive, and that's the outlook that Henk desired for his family. That outlook illustrated the incredible journey of faith God brought Henk through, and it also let his family see the hope in his life and the footprints of the God who saved him.

⎯⎯

Even with the hard times, Henk left his family with hope. He left them a passion for the Word of God and a strong faith that was the echo of Jan's. Christ had entered their lives, and the Holy Spirit had empowered them to do their part and to continue on with hope even after Henk left this world.

While some preach that if we do our part, God will do His, Henk left an understanding with his family that it starts with God first. God *already* did His part, Henk taught; they must only respond.

"Most people wait until they run out of gas and then expect God to bring the gas can," Alton comments on this. "If you engage God at the beginning, He walks it out through you. It's a whole different process. We must engage Him *pre* rather than *post*—before we start out, instead of after we run out of our strength."

"The Bible talks about working hard," Johanna says of her mother, "so she does that. But the other thing she does is give to missions, because that's a great debt we owe." Jan takes great joy in giving extravagantly for her income, truly a modern version of the widow that Jesus commended to His disciples.

The entire family shares Jan's love of missions. "Isn't that something?" Jan says in wonder. "From where I came from and my husband came from, that now our children are all about missions?" When she speaks of it, she becomes excited, a twinkle in her sharp, dark eyes.

Johanna remembers a time when she jokingly remarked to someone that her mother acted like she was the only person who had ever been saved. After saying that, "I just got a strong impression of, 'Why don't you just leave that alone? She is praising God!'"

She adds with a laugh, "Why shouldn't all of us go back and remember all the incredible things that God has done in our lives?"

Remembering what God has done truly is an important element of faith the whole family understands. As such hard workers, it's possible for the family to think they have achieved everything through their own hard work and discipline. "We could forget that we should always be grateful to God," Johanna sums up.

But the Rijfkogels know how important it is to remember that all people depend totally on God, because as Henk's passing showed, no one is granted anything—not even one more day. Henk lost his family in one day to a tragic event, and later his family lost him in one day to an accident. Afterward, the family lived in the daily knowledge that they were not guaranteed tomorrow. Dependence on God defined their values. Remembering God's miracles and daily provision allowed Jan and the children to cast vision into the future.

Although the children all appreciate the faith of their parents, they also feel their family story illustrates that God does not always have to do the miraculous to work miracles. They feel their lives show that as they did the mundane things of life in obedience, God took care of them. At times they faced doubts or obstacles, but they exercised an often-overlooked spiritual discipline of remembering what God had done in the past to gain the courage to press on into the future. If God did it back then, they reasoned, they could trust Him with the future instead of living in fear.

God's role in Jan's story convincingly demonstrated to the entire family that He cares intimately for each person. "He's a personal God," as Johanna puts it. "He is not just our buddy; God is just and sovereign. But He is also loving and relational, and He will get down in the messes of our lives with us." The God of the Bible is attentive to His world and the cry of His people.

The same is true for you. Trouble will come. It is a normal part of life. The Rijfkogels would ask you, "What will you do with it?"

It is their fervent hope that you can look at this story, which played out over many decades, and see God's hand. God's faithfulness is not something unique to the Rijfkogels. The same God who was with them is the same God you can turn to—today and in the future.

The whole family hopes that this story inspires faith and hope in you. But do not forget that sometimes that requires taking a risk. You must trust God. Trust is not an emotion. Trust is an *action*. Trust is obedience to the ways of the Lord.

Johanna can look back and think about all she faced in life with the understanding that, in many ways, what she went through did not compare to the difficulties her mother faced. In the same way, she knows her own child may not fully understand what the Rijfkogel family went through—from moving to America to pulling together after Henk's death.

"The point isn't how much each of us goes through," Johanna asserts. "It's that, through it all, *we depended on God.* We can get away from that all too quickly, and the older I get, the more I see that."

To her children, Jan reminds, "I gave you kids to God, and the only thing I prayed for is that you would serve Him in spirit and in truth and that you would obey His commandments." The whole family recognizes that the power of prayer is not to be overlooked. Her children look back at things Jan has said for years and recognize the hallmarks of her remarkable, ever-fresh faith.

Jan's hope and prayer was not that her children's road be perfect, for she knew that in this life, trouble comes.

So the question always returns: *What will you do with your troubles?*

You stand at a crossroads as you finish this book. You can consider this as merely an uplifting story and a quick, inspiring read of one family's journey. Or, you can see that principles of praise and thanksgiving, of trusting God, of resolute faith, and of hard work turned what could have been a family dogged by tragedy into a family known for triumph.

What will you do with your own troubles? Jan offers an answer.

Start with thanksgiving and praise.

Epilogue

Two threads stretch through time. One follows the course set by God before time began, a thread drawn taut from Genesis to eternity, leading to the arms of the Father Himself.

The other thread is the course that man plots for himself, as he struggles to create and guide his own destiny. It is a kinked and tangled thread, knotted up by mankind's fumbling attempts to straighten it out. And for all its twists and turns, it leads nowhere.

We can follow but one thread at a time. Henk Rijfkogel and Jan Nio Oei grasped like confused blind people at the tangled thread of destiny, and their struggles multiplied. But when they finally turned themselves over to the course of God's plan, they found the rich fulfillment of life well lived.

Yes, there are imponderables. Henk Rijfkogel was snuffed out in his prime, with no clear explanation. And yet, as the Author of our destinies, God owes us no explanations.

We do know that God weaves no destruction into the fabric of His children's lives. "And we know that all things work together for good to them that love God, to them who are the called according to his purpose" (Romans 8:28). The thread of God's will is straight and true.

God loves his own. He loves you. If the lives of Henk and Jan Rijfkogel communicate any message at all, it is the message of God's unfailing love…of His care for both the tiny details of your life—and the grand course of your destiny.

Products

by Alton Garrison

Rekindle Your Hope For An American Revival

In *Hope in America's Crisis: The Future of Missions in America*, Alton Garrison explores the complicated issues and the missional opportunities for every Christian in his or her community. Defining three misperceptions that hamper the church's effectiveness, he suggests ways that believers can overcome them and stand together for national revival. Paper. 144 pages. Available at www.altongarrison.com and www.myhealthychurch.com.

by Alton Garrison

Discover how to produce transformed, godly disciples who circle around to draw others to Christ. This handbook will challenge you to evaluate your own spiritual walk as well as explore the various stages of discipleship — from knowing Christ to becoming a mature leader who disciples others. A special section covers discipling children, youth, families, and people of diverse ethnicities. Paper. 286 pages. Available at www.altongarrison.com, www.myhealthychurch.com, and www.amazon.com.

About the Author

Johanna Garrison was born in Holland to a Dutch father and a Chinese mother and immigrated to the United States at ten years of age. She received her Bachelor of Music Education from Evangel University and has served as a teacher, administrator, conference speaker, and mentor. In addition, she has partnered with her husband, Alton, in multiple ministry positions including evangelist and pastor as well as serving with him in his offices as Superintendent of the Arkansas District, Executive Director of U.S. Missions, and Assistant General Superintendent of the Assemblies of God. Johanna and her husband have one daughter, Lizette, who is married and has a son, Cade. The Garrison's reside in southwest Missouri.

You may contact Johanna at:

Alton Garrison Ministries, Inc.
P.O. Box 64
Ozark, MO 65721
Phone: 417.234.7601
E-mail: GarrisonAGM@aol.com
www.altongarrison.com